CREATIVITY AND GOD

CREATIVITY AND GOD

A Challenge to Process Theology

Robert C. Neville

A Crossroad Book

THE SEABURY PRESS · NEW YORK

1980
The Seabury Press
815 Second Avenue
New York, N.Y. 10017

Printed in the United States of America

Library of Congress Cataloging in Publication Data
Neville, Robert C   Creativity and God.
Includes bibliographical references and index.
1. Process theology. 2. God. I. Title.
BT83.6.N48   231   79–25655
ISBN 0–8164–0120–9

Grateful acknowledgment is made to the following publishers for permission to use the material listed:

Cambridge University Press and Macmillan Publishing
Co., Inc. for excerpts from *Process and Reality* by Alfred
North Whitehead. Copyright 1929 by Macmillan Pub-
lishing Co., Inc., renewed 1957 by Evelyn Whitehead.

Harper & Row, Publishers, Inc., for specified excerpts
from *The Reality of God* by Shubert Ogden. Copyright ©
1977 by Shubert M. Ogden. Reprinted by permission of
Harper & Row, Publishers, Inc.

Martinus Nijhoff for excerpts from *The Transcendental
Imagination: An Essay in Philosophical Theology* by
Charles Winquist.

The Westminster Press for Chapter VII, a revised form of
an essay entitled "Pluralism and Finality in Structures of
Existence," which originally appeared in *John Cobb's
Theology in Process*, edited by David Ray Griffin and
Thomas J. J. Altizer. Copyright © 1977 by The Westmin-
ster Press.

For Andrew B. Smither
and Raymond R. Sturgis
"fathers in the faith"

Contents

Preface

Philosophical theology is now enjoying a resurgence of vigor and creativity after a long period of torpor. Although the field has many contributors, at the center is the profound and subtle movement of process theology. No philosophical theologian can fail to take account of Alfred North Whitehead, his heirs and developers. There have been several kinds of response to process theology. The most careful and nuanced so far has been to endorse its basic drift, to interpret and free it from internal difficulties and to develop it into new areas. It is fair to say that process theology constitutes a school, albeit with different schoolmasters. The opposite response has been to treat process theology as a peculiar tradition, different from one's own, and therefore to be noted but rejected because its basic drift carries it into shoals that one's own tradition avoids easily; until very recently this has been the Thomist reaction, for instance. There are also theologians whose backgrounds are eclectic and whose responses to process theology are appreciative borrowings of this or that aspect; but such thinkers do not often respond to process theology in its integrity as a system. An important need still exists for a systematic and sympathetic critique of process theology from an outside standpoint that has a philosophical project with an independent momentum of its own.

With respect to the problem of God, this book attempts to address that need. My credentials for occupying the requisite critical standpoint were called to my attention by comments on previous writings. Gene Reeves and Delwin Brown noted in 1971 that the "most recent challenge to process theology is Robert Neville's claim that Whitehead's metaphysical theology leaves unanswered the more fundamental questions of ontology, resulting in an inadequacy that is both philosophical and religious."[1] Their discussion drew attention to certain central but critical connections between process theology and my own line of thinking. Since that time I have become increasingly aware of the power of process philosophy in general, while also becoming more clearly distant from it. This book, then, is an attempt to provide a sustained critique of process theism, in its roots and at least some branches, from a standpoint at one with Whitehead in appreciation of speculative philosophy, neighboring in general cosmology and opposed regarding the conception of God.

Because this study may be of use to students of process theology, I have quoted extensively from certain of Whitehead's central passages in the first chapter. In succeeding chapters I have tried as much as possible to focus on single and available sources from the authors discussed in order to aid the reader in making a knowledgeable entry into the dialogue. Portions of the following chapters appeared in altered form in *International Philosophical Quarterly*, *Proceedings of the American Catholic Philosophical Association*, *Process Studies*, *Southern Journal of Philosophy* and *John Cobb's Theology in Process*, edited by Thomas J. J. Altizer and David Ray Griffin (Philadelphia: Westminster, 1977).

I am grateful to more conferences, discussions and individuals than can be mentioned here for comments on this work. Particularly, I would like to thank The Center for Process Studies, ably guided by John Cobb and David Griffin; the Society for the Study of Process Philosophies, directed by George Allan with help from William Hamrick and others; the Process and Praxis Group, an offshoot of the first two groups; and the New Haven Theological Discussion Group, mentored by Stephen Crites and Louis Mink. As to individuals, it will be apparent that this book is part of an ongoing dialogue with Lewis S. Ford, a critic of great mind and soul and without ego; my thanks for continuing discussions also with Thomas J. J. Altizer, Robert Brumbaugh, David R. Griffin, Ray L. Hart, David Hall, Gordon Kaufman, Peter Manchester, Wayne Proudfoot, Sung-bae Park, Jay Schulkin, John E. Smith, William Sullivan, Owen Thomas and George Wolf, as well as with those whose work is discussed explicitly in the text. A very central debt is owed to Paul Weiss in these matters, who has always pushed me to independence.

A note about the context of inquiry. Serious thinking must originate in one's private moments when the problems one takes up and those one sets aside are one's own responsibility. Not to acknowledge this is without warrant to cast responsibility onto some inchoate and irresponsible community. Lame excuses about fashionable intellectual options and "the state of the art" are not to be tolerated. On the other hand, one has not accomplished the work of serious thinking unless the thoughts are made public, available and vulnerable to the community, and dissociated from the special meanings of one's own personal creative intellectual life. In an important sense, the public character of thinking has not individuals but communities for its "subject." An individual's contribution is always a partial thought, a hypothesis whose internal constitution includes the continuing assessments that must be made by others.

So, from the private side, a "sustained critique" inevitably has a polemical odor. As mentioned, my personal stimulation for this essay was the intriguing divergence of process theology from my own. Where this has led the text to draw unnecessarily harsh contrasts or to represent process theology in a poor light without evidence, let my apology be an object lesson about the failure to transcend the privacy of selfish thinking. But from the public side a "sustained critique" itself exemplifies the partiality of individual thinking and serves to take process theology seriously as it cannot be taken seriously by itself and from within. The brief attempts to sketch my own views in contrast to process theism are intended to indicate the perspective from which the critique is made. I hope the community is enriched in some small ways, not only by the existence of the two views, but by a discussion of their dialectical relations.

The book is dedicated to the two people who initiated my first reflections on theology and religion.

Robert C. Neville
Centerport, New York
May 24, 1979

CREATIVITY
AND GOD

• I •

Whitehead's God in Theology

There are two reasons to consider Whitehead's conception of God the most important philosophical idea for contemporary theology. First, it is an intimate part of a general philosophical system that, better than any other, restores cosmology to its rightful place in our intellectual concerns. The revolution in the conception of nature and of nature's unity with human affairs that has been wrought by Whitehead's theory of causation should be accepted, I believe. If his conception of God is mistaken, as I also believe, we are obliged to remove it from his philosophy with great care.[1]

Second, and more important, Whitehead's conception of God forces us to reconsider our religious experience, assaying again which elements are basic and which merely appear basic because of the commitments of some interpretive scheme. In a world society where one tradition's experience must contest with the experience of alien cultures, nothing could be more important for theology.

I

Whitehead did not create his conception of God solely as an implication of his cosmology. Rather, it arose from many sides of his systematic thinking, most of which focused on reflections about nature, experience and history. In his brilliant *Religion in the Making*, Whitehead provided an interpretation of religion as a civilizing of the universal dimensions of experience through the cultivation of exquisite intensities of emotion. The role of the metaphysical conception of God, in this context, is to rationalize and thereby to articulate and preserve those emotional intensities which are experienced as the greatest value. As he concluded in *Religion in the Making:*

> God is that function in the world by reason of which our purposes are directed to ends which in our own consciousness are impartial as to our own interests. . . . He is that element in virtue of which the attainment of such a value for others transforms itself into a value for ourselves. . . . The consciousness which is individual in us, is universal in him: the love which is partial in us is all-embracing in him. Apart from him there could be no world, because there could be no adjustment of individuality. . . . He is not the world, but the valuation of the world. In abstraction from the course of events, this valuation is a necessary metaphysical function. Apart from it, there could be no definite determination of limitation required for attainment. . . . The present type of order in the world has arisen from an unimaginable past, and it will find its grave in an unimaginable future. There remains the inexhaustible realm of abstract forms, and creativity, with its shifting character ever determined afresh by its own creatures, and God, upon whose wisdom all forms of order depend.[2]

In *Process and Reality,* Whitehead's definitive systematic statement, he characterized God in the following terms:

> In the first place, God is not to be treated as an exception to all metaphysical principles, invoked to save their collapse. He is their chief exemplification. Viewed as primordial, he is the unlimited conceptual realization of the absolute wealth of potentiality. In this aspect, he is not *before* all creation, but *with* all creation. But, as primordial, so far is he from "eminent reality," that in this abstraction he is "deficiently actual"—and this in two ways. His feelings are only conceptual and so lack the fulness of actuality. Secondly, conceptual feelings, apart from complex integration with physical feelings, are devoid of consciousness in their subjective forms. . . . His conceptual actuality at once exemplifies and establishes the categoreal conditions. The conceptual feelings, which compose his primordial nature, exemplify in their subjective forms their mutual sensitivity and their subjective unity of subjective aim. These subjective forms are valuations determining the relative relevance of

eternal objects for each occasion of actuality. He is the lure for feeling, the eternal urge of desire. . . . But God, as well as being primordial, is also consequent. He is the beginning and the end. He is not the beginning in the sense of being in the past of all members. He is the presupposed actuality of conceptional operation, in unison of becoming with every other creative act. Thus by reason of the relativity of all things there is a reaction of the world on God. The completion of God's nature into fulness of physical feeling is derived from the objectification of the world in God. . . . One side of God's nature is constituted by his conceptual experience. This experience is the primordial fact in the world, limited by no actuality which it presupposes. It is therefore infinite, devoid of all negative prehensions. This state of his nature is free, complete, primordial, eternal, actually deficient, and unconscious. The other side originates with physical experience derived from the temporal world, and then acquires integration with the primordial side. It is determined, incomplete, consequent, "everlasting," fully actual, and conscious. His necessary goodness expresses the determination of his consequent nature.[3]

Whitehead summed up his magnificent vision with these psalmic antistrophes:

It is as true to say that God is permanent and the World fluent, as that the World is permanent and God is fluent.

It is as true to say that God is one and the World many, as that the World is one and God many.

It is as true to say that, in comparison with the World, God is actual eminently, as that, in comparison with God, the World is actual eminently.

It is as true to say that the World is immanent in God, as that God is immanent in the World.

It is as true to say that God transcends the World, as that the World transcends God.

It is as true to say that God creates the World, as that the World creates God.

God and the World are the contrasted opposites in terms of which Creativity achieves its supreme task of transforming disjoined multiplicity, with its diversities in opposition, into concrescent unity, with its diversities in contrast.[4]

I have quoted so extensively from Whitehead because these are among the most important texts in his corpus for the conception of God. Together with the surrounding metaphysics, they have stimulated the most vigorous, novel developments in philosophical theology since the era of genius in the thirteenth and fourteenth centuries. The purpose of this volume is to examine several lines of interpretation, development and application of Whitehead's ideas. As indicated already, my thesis is that Whitehead's conception of God is largely mistaken and that an alternate conception is to be preferred. Yet Whitehead's broader cosmology is still the most plausible conception of nature to be developed. Therefore, the critical rejection of his conception of God must be undertaken from the inside through a careful analysis of its employment by major thinkers in the process tradition.

Lewis S. Ford is one of the most original and circumspect thinkers in that tradition. In an essay called "The Viability of Whitehead's God for Christian Theology," he claims that "from the standpoint of Christian concerns, Whitehead's metaphysics is most distinctive in being a philosophy of creation which does not identify creative power exclusively with God."[5] Creativity lies underneath the contrasted antistrophes of God and World, as quoted above. Ford then claims that "the non-identification of God with creativity or being itself has many distinct advantages for Christian theism," and enumerates the following.

> 1. In creating itself, each creature is exercising a real freedom distinct from God's. Its freedom is not compromised by being also somehow God's action, or by being already known as determinate in God's foreknowledge. . . .
> 2. On this process view every actuality has ultimate significance as contributing to the experience of God. . . . If God's experience were complete and unchanging for all time, there seems no way in which our action could either add or detract from it and hence no way in which concrete meaning can be given to service for the sake of God's glory. . . .
> 3. A plurality of self-creative acts introduces a measure of potential conflict and incompatibility, which is the mark of evil. God is responsible for the ideals whereby the actions of the world might be co-ordinated, but the world is responsible for all physical actualiza-

tion, for its good and for its evil. . . . Above all, the non-identification of God with creativity exempts God from the responsibility for evil.

4. If both God and the world share in a common creativity, there is a mutual solidarity between them whereby God's agency can be discerned in the activity of the world. . . . The Biblical account of creation illuminates the process of evolution once it is understood as the gradual emergence of order out of chaos through divine guidance rather than as the ontological production of being out of non-being.

5. If God and finite actualities are all alike instances of creativity such that God is also a being and not being-itself, then our knowledge of God can be metaphysically intelligible without recourse to the more desperate strategies of indirect prediction. God becomes no longer an exception to the metaphysical principles but their chief exemplification. God's mystery is not thereby affronted, but discovered in its proper place, not so much at the limits of human intelligibility as in the depths of self-creative freedom.

6. If as a result of non-divine creativity God's experience is contingent upon worldly actualization, then this responsive action toward the world is also contingent. . . . Reason ascertains all it can about God, but in recognizing that there must be contingent aspects in God, it knows that it cannot determine what these are in concrete fact. Here we must appeal to the particularities of God's action in history, to the records of the evolutionary process for God's dealing with nature, and to the records of man's encounter with God for his dealings with man in sacred scripture.[6]

In this long quotation, Ford presents most of the major advantages theologians have seen in process theology. We shall have occasion to recur to them in various guises in the following chapters. But this chapter shall begin the direct discussion, starting with Ford's theme that Whitehead's uniqueness lies in separating God from creativity. Under this rubric shall be considered arguments concerning human freedom, the intrinsic significance of finite beings, evil, the creation of the metaphysical categories, divine finitude and whether a finite God is necessarily part of a larger, more worshipful whole. Next shall be considered Ford's arguments to prove that God can know incomplete phases of an actual occasion's concrescence, that is, that God can know a person in the subjective process of becoming. The final consideration shall be of persons' grasp of the presence of God.

II

The first consideration is a clarification of the contrast intended in claiming God is not to be identified with the ultimate principle of creativity. The alternative I shall defend is not that God *is* to be identified with creativity. Theravada Buddhists might defend this, arguing that the only ultimate reality is the ceaseless flux of forms having neither worshipfulness nor character apart from the train of evanescent patterns.

My own alternative is that God is creator of everything determinate, creator of things actual as well as of things possible. Apart from the relative nature the divinity gives itself as creator in creating the world, God is utterly transcendent. The why or wherefore of the original creative act is mysterious, as Ford notes. But, relative to the world as creator, God is present to each creature in the divine creative act giving determinate being; and the world itself is a normative expression of the creator, undetachable from the divine creative reality. The creator, the act and the expression form the rudiments of a philosophical trinitarianism. Contrasting with God's *ontological* creativity, we can distinguish the *cosmological* creativity exercised by creatures constituting the world. With Whitehead I agree (1) that the course of the world is characterized by events of harmonizing multiplicities into unities and (2) that the reality of the event for itself is the processive becoming of the unity; I accept Whitehead's categoreal obligations for this process of cosmological creativity.[7] What I call cosmological creativity, the only sort Whitehead acknowledges, is a descriptive generalization of the character of events; the reality of the events is accounted for with the ontological creativity of God the Creator.[8] God is the immediate creator of the novel values or patterns by which an event is constituted as the harmonizing of a multiplicity. Since the real being of an occasion is the becoming of a harmonized integration of the multiplicity, its components stem either immediately from God or from what it prehends; since what it prehends are other occasions, themselves analyzable into novel and prehended features, it can be suggested that every feature at some time in the present or past is or was a spontaneous novel pattern or value immediately created by God. Thus God is the creator of every determinate thing, each in its own occasion of spontaneous appearance. In contrast to God's ontological creativity, cosmological creativity is the descriptive fact that the spontaneity, in occasions brings unity out of multi-plicity.[9]

The point of this lengthy sketch of an alternative to Whitehead is that many of the virtues advertised for his conception of God are also possessed, perhaps more satisfactorily, by the alternative, as will be illustrated in some of the topics discussed below.

1. Human independence or ontological freedom from God is the virtue most often appealed to in the Whiteheadian conception of God, standing first in Ford's list of virtues. The point is, be-cause God is not identified with creativity as such, having only God's own specification of it (other finite individuals having their own specifications of it), people have their own independent being, underived from God, however interdependent God and the world are in other respects. And because being in this case means a specific act of creativity, harmonizing a given multiplic-ity into the individual's own concrete self, the independent being is independent self-determination, or freedom. Whitehead ac-counts for God's influence on other actual occasions with the doctrine that God contributes in the initial phase of concrescence a value orienting the subjective aim of the occasion: In later phases the occasion can modify the subjective aim according to self-determined emphasis.[10] Allowing all this for the moment, I want to point out that this kind of freedom is a mixed blessing.

First, Whitehead and Ford must acknowledge God to be an ex-ternal limit on human freedom in the same sense that other exter-nal things limit freedom. All objective things limit freedom in that they are given as initial data required to be harmonized in the prehending occasion's concrescence. God's datum is so important as to determine the initial state of the subjective aim. Whereas fi-nite occasions determine themselves, God is rather like a smother-mother, structuring all possibilities and continually in-sisting on values of her own arbitrary choice. Considering crea-tures' immortality in God's life, in the long run there is a metaphysical guarantee that people cannot damn themselves, and the possibility of self-damnation seems to me a touchstone of freedom.

The Whiteheadian answer is that the limitations contributed to an occasion by the world and by God are not negative, in any sense limiting freedom, but rather positive values; limitation is essential to value. But freedom for Whiteheadians is supposed to be an occasion's own creativity in determining its own final limitation within the range of possibilities inherent in the initial data. That is, an occasion chooses what limitation or value it will become, given the alternate possibilities for harmonizing the initial data. Insofar as God determines that value through the subjective aim in the initial data, the occasion's own choice is depleted. And, if God continues to determine modifications of the subjective aim through the process, it is hard to see any freedom of choice left. Even if there is always a residue of self-determined emphasis left to the occasion, the *function* of God is still to force feed a person's intentions even more powerfully than other things do.

The way to get around this objection is to say that God's contribution of possibilities and values is somehow *identical* with that occasion's process of self-determination. But this would require the denial of the ontological independence of God and finite occasions. If God's contribution of a spontaneous value defining an occasion's becoming is *identical* with that occasion's free adoption of the value, then for God to create the value at that point is for the occasion to be self-determining. We could claim a person's choice is determined by another in this case only if we said, in fact, that God's being as creator is other than the person's free process as creature. The conception of God as creator denies such an ontological difference, although Whitehead's theory must hold to it. The problem for the creation view, admittedly, is to articulate the right sense in which God is not ontologically distinct from creatures and yet is their creator, ontologically independent of them.[11]

From the standpoint of religious and ethical experience, I submit, *both* human self-determination and divine determination of men are felt in the same act. Furthermore, as Job found out, it is misleading to interpret God's control of things with the model of a supercreature's control of things.

2. Concerning a creature's intrinsic significance, the second of the virtues Ford cites for Whitehead's view, an analogous objection holds: If the value which the creature attains is contributed forcibly by an ontologically independent God, its significance is

intrinsically *located* in actuality but extrinsically derived and determined. Ford's argument itself focuses rather on a creature's intrinsic contribution to value in the universe as preserved by God; without ontological independence, he says, our experience could neither add to nor detract from God's. But ontological independence is not the issue: a creator God who creates a person intrinsically possessing such and such a value has precisely that value in the divine creative experience; were God not to create that person, God would lack the value of being creator-in-that-person. The intrinsic significance of creatures is strictly correlative to the values in God's experience, on the creationist view, and this is so whether the value comes cosmologically to be actualized through the creature's own choice or through blind antecedent determination. Since God's creative act creates temporal determinations and is not temporally determined itself except in specific reference to temporal things, the issue of a creature's adding something to God's experience not possessed before is meaningful only from the creature's point of view. And from that point of view God is not specifically creator of such and such a valuable creature "until" it temporally comes to be.

3. Concerning evil, the Whiteheadian view indeed makes finite actual occasions responsible for the evil resulting from their own choices, moral or submoral. Of course, to the extent that people's choices are hedged in by divinely urged possibilities and values, as argued above, the choices can hardly be said to be the people's own; who can be responsible for resisting an Infinite Nudge?

But suppose evil is chosen only by people, and only in independence from God. Why should we want in the first place to exempt God from responsibility for evil? Because of an antecedent commitment to God's goodness. But to deny God responsibility by denying divine causal agency is not to lend *support* to the doctrine of divine goodness; it only strikes down a counter argument. And the price of this move is to make the actual course of events *irrelevant* to God's moral character; this goes counter to the religious feeling that God's moral character is *revealed* in events, for better or worse.

Futhermore, it makes the doctrine of God's goodness itself an ad hoc hypothesis of the metaphysical theory, not something with experiential warrant. If God's primordial decision regarding

values and limitation in general is at root arbitrary, as Whitehead
says it is, then it is only coincidence if God is metaphysically
good, this being an arbitrary decision God makes in determining
the metaphysical principles to which divinity must conform. Although Ockham's razor is a dangerous weapon, I think the
simpler doctrine would be that, if God is to be judged by moral
categories (remember Job), the divine character is only as good
as experience shows it to be as creator of just this world, and no
more. God is a good creator insofar as the creation is good, and
beyond that there is no reason to judge. This should be admitted
whether or not one maintains that God creates the whole world or
only the metaphysical principles (Whitehead's position).

4. Concerning that last point, I agree with Ford in singling out
Whitehead's statement that God's "conceptual actuality at once
exemplifies and establishes the categoreal conditions."[12] This is
what Whitehead meant to say, I believe, and Ford is acute in
showing this renders a valid sense of actuality; God's primordial
nature is the result as well as the reality of *decision*.

But I also fear the doctrine is untenable, and that Whitehead is
mistaken. It is the character of a process of concrescence that, at
any phase short of the final satisfaction, the unity of prehensions
is partly indeterminate; before the satisfaction, then, the final satisfaction cannot be determinately exemplified. Especially, it cannot be said that the metaphysical categories are normatively
binding on what is possible for God *before* they achieve their satisfactory determination.

It might be countered that the metaphysical principles are determined in their full extent in the next-to-initial stage of God's
primordial envisagement, and that later stages are more determinate resolutions of possible relations within possibilities left open
by the metaphysical principles. But in this case there either is or
is not a reason why God decides on the metaphysical principles:
If there is a reason, the principles are normative in the initial
phase of God's decision and are therefore uncreated; if there is no
reason, the principles being ultimately arbitrary as Whitehead
says, then they do not determine the possibilities in the first move
from the initial stage of envisagement to the next in which the
principles appear and that first move does *not* exemplify them.

It is possible to say, as the doctrine that God is ontological creator does, that God creates the determinate metaphysical principles or categoreal conditions; indeed, Whitehead is right in saying that anything complex is the result of decision (in this case, divine decision). Furthermore, the principles describe God as the God who creates a world exhibiting these principles, including those articulating the divine created relation to the world. But it makes no sense to say the principles are norms for the concrescence of God's primordial decision before they are created. Whereas the metaphysical principles determine the difference between possibility and impossibility for a *finite* occasion's concrescence, and the categoreal obligations in fact are rules for concrescing, God's primordial creation of the principles cannot be called a concrescence in any way determined by the principles created.

5. Let me repeat my appreciation of Ford's demonstration of God's conceptual infinity on Whitehead's view, and the peculiar actuality this entails.[13] This takes most of the starch out of the usual attacks on the finitude of Whitehead's God in the divine consequent nature. It should be noted, however, that if one rejects Whitehead's account of freedom, of the intrinsic significance of finite occasions and of evil, much of the reason for saying God is finite in having a separate specification of creativity is taken away.

Furthermore, concerning the infinite side, there is a theoretical difficulty in saying whether the primordial decision is once accomplished and ever after objectively immortal or is rather everlastingly concrescing, never complete. Whitehead says both, and Ford cites both passages.[14] I shall deal with this theoretical difficulty in treating the problem of our knowledge of God. Here I want to flag the point that the real onus of the charge that God should not be finite is the subordinate status a finite God would have relative to any whole including God plus the other ontologically independent beings, a point that will be developed at length below.

6. Ford is correct to point out that God is not finite with respect to creativity in Whitehead's scheme, since creativity is indeterminate apart from concrete specifications. He is also correct that God's conceptual nature excludes no possibility or achieved value; God feels the achieved value of every finite occasion with

the same subjective form with which the finite occasion in its own satisfaction feels itself. But God's finitude does contrast exclusively with the subjective process of concrescence in each temporal occasion; this is required for the mutual ontological independence of divine and temporal free decisions. Whereas in consequent nature God might contain the value of the whole world, in no way does God contain the creative activity of other creatures. The ontological whole includes God plus the world.

Whitehead's apt description for God plus the world, ontologically considered, is the "solidarity" of God and world in the creative advance. There are marked similarities to Hegel's Absolute Spirit. The crucial question is whether the solidarity of the advance is not more divine, more worshipful, than Whitehead's God. Hegel would say yes. By virtue of the very solidarity, God and the world are mutually dependent, and religious experience seems to prefer the relatively more independent. Whitehead could counter that his God, and not the world, is the creative source of the metaphysical principles, of all relevant possibilities and of all possible values, maintaining the achieved values against loss. But the answer to this is that the complete creative advance is creator not only of all God's contribution, but also of the concrete achievement of finite value in the temporal decisions. The very antistrophes of God and world quoted earlier mark a total holiness superior to the dependencies of the divine pole. There may be difficulties with the quasipantheism of the claim that the creative advance is most divine, or with Hegel's Absolute Spirit. But pantheism has a solid footing in religious experience, as nearly every religious tradition exemplifies. In essence, I think nothing short of the ground or principle of the whole of things is supreme enough to be worshiped.

This concludes the initial discussion of points raised by Ford's general thesis that there is an advantage in distinguishing God from creativity or being-itself. Dispute about these advantages of Whitehead's conception will be themes for variations in several of the chapters that follow with discussions of different authors. Two more critical themes may be stated, however, before moving on to the specific variations. The first is whether Whitehead's conception of God adequately addresses the question of God's knowledge of human beings; the second is how people can know God.

III

One of the distinct advantages often cited for Whitehead's conception is that, since God is conceived as an individual actual entity (or a society of such entities according to Charles Hartshorne's view) with an intrinsically conceptual component, it makes sense to say God knows the world, particularly human beings. Doubtless there is initial plausibility in this suggestion compared with alternatives.

The conception of God as pure act, for instance, does not allow God to be thought of as sufficiently determined by what the divine knowledge contains in order to learn anything; in the classic formula (to be discussed in Chapter Five), the world is relative to God as pure act but the divine pure act is not relative to God.[15]

The conception of God as creator *ex nihilo*, in its turn, can call God "a knower" only by a thinly stretched analogy; being indeterminate as apart from the world, God cannot have knowledge that is about an external world interior to a divine nature; this theory must say that divine knowledge is the same as divine creating (Immanuel Kant's position).[16]

What about Whitehead's conception? The problem is that, in the Whiteheadian conception, God can know, feel or appreciate only people's deeds as done, finished; God cannot prehend them in their hearts, in their processes of becoming. The reason is that God is related to people *only* by prehending them and being prehended by them, and one can prehend only an objective reality, a satisfaction at the end of becoming. Whitehead was clear about there being no prehension of contemporaries in the sense of prehending the becoming of another entity not yet objectively come to be.

Recognizing this difficulty, one might supplement Whitehead with the doctrine that God can prehend the *in*complete phases of a temporal occasion's concrescence. The rationale would be that God can prehend anything determinate and, although the multiplicity in those incomplete phases are not determinately together, they are determinately individual and can be known as such. The reason that nondivine occasions are unable to prehend incomplete phases (according to this argument) is that they must wait upon the extensive perspective of the concrescing occasion to be completed for the occasion to be distinguished from the actual world from which the prehending entities arose. Since God is not extensive, being unable in fact to make the negative prehensions necessary to stake out a perspective, God need not wait upon the concrescing occasion to stake out a location of its own. This is an ingenious argument.[17]

Whitehead did not make this move himself. For him the incomplete phases of an occasion are not actual, and only actual things can be prehended. The reason they are not actual is that they are not completely determinate and therefore cannot be objective. Whitehead wrote, "An entity is actual when it has significance for itself. By this is meant that an actual entity functions in respect to its own determination. Thus an actual entity combines self-identity with self-diversity."[18] I take this to mean that an entity is actual only with respect to its self-identity achieved in the completed satisfaction. Whitehead further wrote:

> The actual entity is the enjoyment of a certain quantum of physical time. But the genetic process is not the temporal succession: such a view is exactly what is denied by the epochal theory of time. Each phase in the genetic process presupposes the entire quantum, and so does each feeling in each phase. The subjective unity dominating the process forbids the division of that extensive quantum which originates with the primary phase of the subjective aim. The problem dominating the concrescence is the actualization of the quantum *in solido*. The quantum is that standpoint in the extensive continuum which is consonant with the subjective aim in its original derivation from God.[19]

I take this to mean that there is no possibility of *existentially* separating the incomplete phases from each other or from the whole. There is no existential time in which an occasion's incomplete parts exist without the whole. The division of an occasion into phases is an abstraction made from the whole, and only the whole is a *res vera*. If God were to prehend an incomplete phase, it would only be the *idea* of an incomplete phase, not the part of an individual different from God. In actuality, there is an event moving from a multiplicity, in which the new individual is completely future, to a new unity in which the new individual is completely determinate, and there is no actuality to be prehended in between. It might be argued that the incomplete phases are indeed not temporal, but eternal, and that God does not prehend them in the temporal consequent nature, but in the eternal primordial nature; but this is to give up the thesis that God prehends temporal people in their hearts.

Perhaps a more perspicuous way of putting this objection is that, if the incomplete phases of an occasion can be abstracted out to be prehended, the occasion itself is not being prehended; the occasion *is not itself* until its satisfaction is achieved. Although the satisfaction is contained in the subjective aim as a *potentiality* for actualization in the incomplete phases, the subjective aim with potentiality is precisely not objective for prehension, although a propositional statement of it is. To claim that the subjective aim in incomplete phases is prehendable as such is to deny process, the essence of Whitehead's insight, reducing an occasion to a succession of objectifiable patterns. The genetic *analysis* of an actual entity can abstract the process into such a succession of patterns, but this is an abstraction explicitly prescinding from the reality of the creative process of the concrete event.

This ingenious argument succeeds only at the expense of giving up the epochal theory of time, the doctrine of events and the vibratory interpretation of existence, crucial elements in Whitehead's metaphysics. My own preference is to maintain those doctrines of nature and to jettison the Whiteheadian conception of God in favor of a different view of the world's presence to God. To turn this preference into an argument, however, the coherence of Whitehead's own conception of God as related to the world must be examined—the topic of Chapter Two. But it must be admitted here that in Whitehead's conception, God can not know people in the subjective immediacy of their heart.

IV

The obverse side of the problem of God's knowledge of the world and the human heart is the problem of our knowledge of

God. For reasons that will be discussed in Chapter Six, Whitehead and his followers are right in interpreting God's knowledge
of us and our knowledge of God in causal terms, not transcendental ones. But the question is whether the relevant causation is
between actual entities or between actual entities on the one hand
and the creator of all determinate things on the other.

Concerning human knowledge of God, most religions exhibit
something of the feeling that God is experienced at the center of
one's own heart, that Atman is Brahman, that God is closer to us
than we are to ourselves. As Paul Tillich pointed out in his classic
paper, "Two Types of Philosophy of Religion," the approach to
God as an Other is always complemented by the approach to God
at the depths of one's own being.[20] Whitehead's view, precisely
because of the emphasis on separate acts of creativity for God and
finite occasions, allows God only to be felt as other. In Whitehead's terms, God is prehended as an item among the initial data
of an occasion, just the way the rest of the world is prehended, in
the form of a hybrid physical prehension providing the orienta-
tion of the occasion's subjective aim. But Whitehead also emphasized that the occasion can modify its subjective aim in
subsequent phases.

One can meet this difficulty head on by claiming that God not
only is prehended among the initial data, but is prehended in
subsequent phases as presenting the best possibility, taking into
account each modification and decision of the occasion. Thus God
is at the heart of the whole of the subjective process of actualization, not just at the beginning when the rest of the world is presented.

Against this suggestion, however, there are two objections.
The first is allied with the argument concerning God's knowledge
of finite occasions. Just as there are no existent incomplete phases
in finite occasions for God to prehend, so there are none to prehend God; rather, the occasion as an actual whole prehends God
and the world, and this is to be analyzed into prehensions unhar-
monized, which we call the initial stage, and the prehensions
harmonized, which we call the satisfaction, with analytical
components of logical progression toward harmony, which we
call intermediate incomplete phases.

The second objection is that there are grave difficulties with the concept of God required for this suggestion. As remarked before, Whitehead equivocated on whether God's concrescence is something forever in process and never complete or something that has at least some completed and completely determinate decisions. It is clear that for occasions to prehend God, God would have to have some completed and objective presentations. Perhaps these divine valuations, allegedly relevant for each phase in the concrescence of an occasion, are themselves incomplete phases of the one everlasting divine concrescence, determinate disjunctively in relation to the different temporal occasions and phases of occasions, but indeterminate in their ultimate conjunction in the overall experience of God. An intriguing thought!

But how can they be prehended? Even allowing, as has been argued we should not, that an incomplete phase of a temporal occasion is the sort of thing that can prehend, its prehension of God would have to be a hybrid physical prehension. "A hybrid physical prehension has as its datum an antecedent occasion objectified in respect to a conceptual prehension."[21] Whitehead pointed out that this means the mental element prehended—in our case God's valuation—does not itself have a coordinate divisibility; in other words, God need not be prehended as being in space and time, something with which Ford would agree.[22] But it does mean that the divine conception prehended must be *antecedent to the time of the temporal occasion.*

Yet this is impossible for two reasons. First, the temporal occasion itself *has* no time in its incomplete phases, only in its final satisfaction; an incomplete phase is only logically subsequent to the initial phase, not later than it. Second, God's prehended valuation must have *a* time, a date, in order to be antecedent to the occasion's time; in fact, supposing there to be a temporal distinction between the occasion's phases, God's *remedial* valuation would have to be later than God's valuation initially prehended, and earlier than the later phase. So, whereas God does not have to be prehended *as* temporally located, God must be temporally located to be prehended. One might respond that, in the consequent nature, God is in fact temporally located, and that the remedial valuation to be prehended is a contrast schematizing the divine primordial valuation with God's temporal physical prehension of the incomplete phase of the finite occasion. But the incomplete phase is not physical and cannot be temporally prehended. Not only are people incapable of experiencing God in incomplete phases of their becoming, God cannot respond from the divine side in a relevant way to those incomplete phases.

The upshot of this rather technical discussion is that, in Whitehead's conception, God is no more at the heart of human subjectivity than any other thing which enters among the initial data of experience. We considered the suggestion that would have God be prehended not only at the initial stage, but also at each incomplete stage within the concrescence, remedially luring each modification of the initial subjective aim. But this suggestion seems incompatible with the main lines of Whitehead's cosmology. And so the Whiteheadian conception of God appears to leave the knowledge of God by human beings at best a somewhat external affair, contrary to the widespread experience of God as that most real part of ourselves.

V

This chapter has surveyed some of the major advantages claimed for Whitehead's conception of God in philosophical theology and has rehearsed a line of objections to be developed in the following chapters with regard to the emphases of various Whiteheadians. The next step in the argument is to turn from the ways by which the Whiteheadian conception serves the interests of what theologians would like antecedently to say about God, to the coherence of the conception itself. Does Whitehead's conception make the divine life comprehensible? Perhaps at some deeper level the conception surmounts the difficulties introduced so far.

· II ·

Process and
Eternity within God

If the central point of Whitehead's contribution to philosophical theology has been clearly to distinguish God from creativity, then two related consequences follow for the conception of God. God is to be conceived as subject to the same metaphysical structures that characterize other things within the creative process by which all actual things are real. Therefore, the same principles apply to God as apply to finite things, although perhaps in unique ways. Moreover, the nature of process itself must be exhibited within God, contrary to many classical views of God as eternal, because process characterizes all things subject to creativity.

Within process cosmology there are two aspects to process. One has to do with the "process" from one occasion to the next and is extremely important for understanding order and disorder within the cosmos. Applied to the conception of God, the "transition" aspect of process is crucial for those philosophical theologies following Charles Hartshorne which hold that God is not a single actual occasion but a society of occasions. Chapters Four and Five particularly will examine this approach.

The other aspect of process is the coming-to-be of occasions themselves, their subjective arising. Whitehead called the analysis of this coming-to-be "genetic division." For those philosophical theologies that hold God to be a single actual occasion, the only divine process is genetic process, and all problems of coherence of the various elements, primordial and consequent, of God's nature must be accounted for in terms of what appears in genetic division. The approach to the conception of God through the categories of genetic division is the focus of this chapter.

I

This approach seeks accommodation with Whitehead's own texts and with Western conceptions of God more classical than Hartshorne's. As pursued by Lewis S. Ford, it focuses on the primacy of the primordial nature of God, the transcendent eternity of the primal creative decision establishing the categoreal conditions (and in fact *all* conditions of absolute generality) and the difference between the divine "spatiality" and the perspectival positions of finite occasions.[1] This direction of process theology has a natural interest in the claim that genetic division analyzes a not exactly temporal but still real succession of phases. According to this claim, God can be said to have a single everlasting concrescence with successive phases. The initial plausibility of this claim lies in Whitehead's clear distinction between temporal relations, which hold between different occasions, and the ordinal relations of "initial," "intermediate" and "final" phases, which are revealed by genetic division within each single occasion. Whereas the process relating concrescences serially is temporal, the process within a single concrescence is not temporal. The difficulties with this position, as Hartshorne's school would emphasize, center around having insufficient successiveness of genetic phases for God to be responsive to changes deriving from the freedom of individual occasions in the temporally ordered world: God is not supposed to know the outcome of a decision before the decision is made.

Ford has addressed himself directly to the claim for nonphysical (but still temporal) successiveness in the genetic process.[2] He begins by pointing out that the differences between phases in a single occasion cannot be mere differences in complexity of integration. Although the eternal objects descriptive of the different phases may differ only by complexity of integration, to identify the genetic process with its definite eternal objects is to miss the dynamism of the *decisions* involved in the succession of phases.[3] The proposal, then, is that there is a phase of genetic development beyond the initial one for each modification of the initial, divinely given, subjective aim. The subjective aim at each phase provides the subjective unity of all the data at that phase; subjective unity at every phase means only that the data are compatible for synthesis, not that they are completely integrated. Lack of complete integration means the phase is an incomplete one in the whole genetic process. The final phase of satisfaction consists in complete determination where the subjective unity is fulfilled with complete integration or synthesis.[4]

Earlier phases causally influence their successors, according to Ford's hypothesis, but do not completely determine them precisely because "being later" means making further decisions. But what about the sense in which the occasion is supposed to be *causa sui* as a whole? Ford writes: "Now there is only one act of self-actualization, but this one act is genetically (not actually) analyzable into successive decisions having within their particular phases the same properties Whitehead ascribes to the occasion as a whole with respect to decisions."[5] The critical point, of course, is the claim for genetic but not actual analyzability. Ford's position is clear. Each phase is *causa sui* in itself through its decisive modificaton of subjective aim; the final phase or satisfaction completes the *sui generis* creativity of the occasion. But if each phase including the last is *causa sui*, is the occasion as a whole *causa sui?* Of course, answers Ford.

> If we think of the occasion as a whole, we may distinguish between the totality of causal influences inherited from the past actual world and its *causa sui* which is finally expressed in the way it has completely integrated these causal influences (by inclusion and/or exclusion) in the satisfaction. Antecedent phases of concrescence are not *additional* causal influences the occasion must integrate, but the means whereby the *causa sui* expresses itself in this process of actualization. In this sense, then, they are not antecedent causes for the self-causation expressed in the mode of integration of the satisfaction, but the agency whereby that self-causation becomes effective.[6]

But this is to interpret "the occasion *as a whole*" to mean the complete set of phases in the occasion, not the occasion as a singular actual entity whose phases are abstractly, that is, analytically, contained in it.

My interpretation of Ford's position, therefore, is that he construes the temporal character of an extended linear series of occasions to be a series of phases punctuated by demarcations of discontinuity. Some phases are completely determinate, but these are continuous with each other by virtue of mediating phases of incomplete determination moving toward penultimate determination. A single actual occasion is the set of phases beginning with an incompletely determinate phase and ending with the next completely determinate phase, termed the occasion's satisfaction. This interpretation is supported by Ford's terminological suggestions regarding Whitehead's doctrine of supersession. Whitehead said time is one species of supersession, namely, that in which the physical pole of one occasion (its completion in satisfaction) supersedes the physical poles of others and is, in turn, superseded by later occasions. But another species of supersession, according to Whitehead, is that in which there is supersession of mental and physical poles, i.e., of phases, within each occasion. The moral Whitehead draws is "that the category of supersession transcends time, since this linkage [of physical and mental poles within an occasion] is both extratemporal and yet is an instance of supersession."[7] Ford's terminological suggestion is to identify time with supersession as such, distinguishing two species, physical and genetic time.[8] I take this to mean that physical time is the measure of serial order from satisfaction to satisfaction and genetic time is the measure of the phases beginning with the first incompletely determinate one after a satisfaction and moving through the next satisfaction. The advantage Ford urges by this revision of terms is the giving of prima facie weight to the temporal connotations of Whitehead's language about earlier and later phases.

There are two important reasons for believing Ford's interpretation is not what Whitehead meant. The first is it misconstrues what a genetic division is supposed to be and the second is it neglects the distinction between becoming and being, between appearance and reality. I shall deal with these in turn.

According to Whitehead, the analysis of an actual entity into prehensions exhibits the most concrete elements in its nature, and such an analysis is called a division.[9] Genetic analysis is one such kind of division. Now a prehension in any division, including genetic, has all the features of an actual entity itself with an important exception:

> By reason of a certain incomplete partiality, a prehension is only a subordinate element in an actual entity. A reference to the complete actuality is required to give the reason why such a prehension is what it is in respect to its subjective form. This subjective form is determined by the subjective aim at further integration, so as to obtain the "satisfaction" of the completed subject.[10]

I take this to mean, first, that a genetic division is not the analysis of an occasion into phases, but the analysis of an occasion into prehensions. Since a prehension, because of its "certain incomplete partiality," cannot be understood by itself, its subjective form must be explained by reference to the place of the prehension in the whole occasion *as determined in phases.* In other words, the reference to phases in a genetic division is essential only because this is what accounts for the character of a prehension's subjective form; coordinate division, neglecting subjective form, need make no reference to phases.

Second, the thing being divided is the actual entity as a whole; prehensions are that into which it is divided. Of course, we may think of the complete occasion as one harmonized prehension; but this is what is to be analyzed, not an analytical component. The sense in which a prehension is a concrete element divided out of an actual entity requires the prehension to be partial with respect to its subjective form. A complete prehension is undivided and can only be physically felt.

It follows from this, I believe, that incomplete phases of an occasion are themselves abstractions from satisfied occasions. They have no existence in themselves so as to be able to exist earlier than the satisfaction phase. Furthermore, phases are abstract elements of the satisfaction called upon to explain prehensions, and themselves are more abstract than prehensions. If prehensions are partial and require the whole occasion in order to have completely determinate subjective form, so much more do the earlier phases need the completed occasion to exist at all. To speak of an occasion's satisfaction as itself a phase, the last in the genetic process, is only an abstraction derivative from the intention to give a genetic analysis; apart from any division of it, the occasion itself just is its satisfaction or complete determination coming to be and being.

Now it might be argued (although Ford does not do so) that each phase in a genetic process is a pattern of prehensions, the later differing from the earlier in containing certain novel conceptual prehensions. But the prehensions of each phase must be different from those of the other phases by virtue of different subjective forms, just as in Whitehead's view the prehensions of each occasion differ from those of each other by virtue of the same reason. I believe Whitehead wanted to avoid just this proliferation of prehensions beyond necessity in his doctrine of epochal time. The point of the appeal to phases in an epoch is to explain the subjective form of prehensions divided out of the satisfied actual entity. The explanation begins with the whole satisfied entity plus the previous entities that entered into it, and explains the former by phases of decision transforming the latter into it.

My objection to Ford's claim that an earlier phase exists before a later phase, in a genetic sense of "exists before," does not conclude that the difference between phases is merely a matter of complexity of eternal objects. He is certainly right about the dynamism of the process of coming to be, a dynamism not expressed at all in coordinate division except by measurements of energy. Rather, my objection is that he construes earlier phases to be just as real in a temporal sense as the concrete occasion itself, albeit the phases are real in genetic time not physical time.

The second reason for doubting Ford's interpretation, therefore, picks up at this point. The genetic process is one of becoming; the temporal process one of being. Time measures real change; genesis measures the appearance of reality. These are important themes for Whitehead not registered by Ford's interpretation in sufficient depth.

The early phases of concrescence are only the becoming of the concrete fact; therefore they are not anything yet, only the becoming of something. They are not real earlier than the satisfactions because they are not by themselves real. The *reality* ingredient in early phases is only the reality attained by previous occasions present as prehensive data; all the differences between the early phases of an occasion and previous occasions are consti-tuted by the concrescent occasion's *appearances* plus the elimina-tion of some initial data required for objectifying the appearances. What does in fact appear is the new reality in the physical satis-faction of the concrescent occasion; but in the early phases it has not completely appeared and is therefore only mere appearance.

Our language, of course, makes it very difficult to speak of phases of becoming or stages of appearance. The language reflects the Aristotelian bias that subjects must be real substances. In the Aristotelian scheme, growth and development are primarily the unfolding of potentialities in successive phases, each phase of which is itself substantial reality; a squirrel killed before repro-ducing is no less a substance because it ceased to exist before ful-filling the final cause of being a squirrel. It is with philosophical metaphors like Aristotle's in mind that Ford's interpretation of genetic successiveness gains its force. But Whitehead, at least at this point, was more Platonic. Coming to be is not the same as, or composed of, being. To be in a world of change requires coming to be, and having-come-to-be in a world of changes requires in-stant perishing. Being cannot dwell in change except as goal or past fact. These rather general remarks do not prove anything, of course; they only suggest one must live in an Aristotelian world to draw genetic successiveness so close to physical time as to call both time. This is not Whitehead's world.

Now the genetic process is indeed dynamic, a matter of deci-sions. But this is to say, from the standpoint of existent occasions, that occasions can be analyzed as having come to be through dy-namic decision. From that standpoint, there is no dynamism left; everything has been decided except what the future will do. Whitehead's point is not that the dynamics we feel characterizing our experience is an illusion but, rather, that our dynamic experi-ence, our subjective immediacy, is not fully real but only the ap-pearing of reality.

Ford would agree with this last point if only there were no elimination during concrescence. Elimination (which both of us agree does happen) requires a real diminution or perishing of that which is real, he argues. But this diminution or perishing is am-biguous. What happens in elimination is that some datum is elim-inated from objectification in that particular concrescing occasion.

This in no way diminishes the objective immortality of the datum as a *potential* for objectification; it is a potential quite apart from being actually objectified, and is so forever even if always actually eliminated. In no sense does elimination cause the datum to *perish* as a potential. The only thing diminished is the concrescing occasion which no longer can objectify the datum; but even this presumes (falsely) that the occasion "exists" at an early stage possessing the datum, which is lost to a later stage. It is better to say merely that a potential datum is not in the end objectifiable in this particular occasion, given its final determinate character; the reason for this is the decision to eliminate.

When an occasion has appeared, when it has fully come to be, it loses its subjective immediacy, its process of decision, its feeling of self-possession. For the feeling of self-possession consists precisely in deciding on the appearance of one's own reality. Is this to say the realm of decisive, dynamic change is only appearance, not quite real? The answer is *yes*, if care is taken not to substantialize "realm" or to infer there is *no* reality to appearance. Is this to say that the objects *known*, the actual occasions which are known by subjecting them to divisions, are realities, not appearances, in the realm of being, not becoming? Yes. Is it to say the only "knowledge" we have of appearances, of the genetic process of decision and change, is hypothetical, derived as one of an indefinite number of possible divisions of the actual entity? Yes. Familiar Platonic themes.

II

Let us suppose now, however, that Ford's interpretation of Whitehead on successiveness be accepted, and that whatever impulses Whitehead might have had inconsistent with it be excised. What hypothesis could be formed about successiveness in God? God's primordial nature could be admitted to be plainly nontemporal, in fact creative of the categoreal conditions giving definiteness to time.[11] But in relation to the world where God must be relative to physically temporal changes, the divinity can be said to be temporal in the genetic sense although not in the physical sense. Since God's concrescence is never complete it is an everlasting genetically temporal process.

The alleged advantage of this hypothesis is that God is temporal enough to be real earlier than a finite event, so that the event can have a hybrid physical prehension of God deriving its subjective aim, etc., and also later than the event taking the event's unique decisions into account. Since God's time is genetic and not physical, there is no necessity to say God experiences in discrete occasions, a move that leads to the Hartshornean view of God as a society. The hypothesis of genetic time in God presupposes what I called the Aristotelian framework, since within the Platonic framework the claim that God has an everlasting genetic concrescence entails the claim that, with respect to that concrescence, God is always only appearing and never ever really real, a consequence Ford wants to avoid.

The fundamental objection to Ford's hypothesis seems to me its inability to allow God's concrescence any opening to the world. The very meaning of genetic successiveness in contrast to physical time is that after the initial phase the concrescence is closed off from outside influence until it reaches satisfaction; this is necessary to preserve the discontinuity of becoming. If no phase of the divine concrescence is completely determinate as a physical satisfaction, there can be no hybrid physical prehension of God by finite occasions, and hence God cannot contribute subjective aims to the finite temporal process. On the other hand, if the divine concrescence is everlasting, and if data from physically antecedent occasions enter the concrescence only in its initial phase, then God can prehend nothing of the world; God's only data could be the divine primordial nature. God could never pick up *initial* data about a finite occasion because the divine *initial* phase would always have preceded it. If God can neither concresce to satisfaction before any finite occasion nor begin a concrescing experience after one, God is strictly speaking contemporary with everything else and therefore absolutely isolated. This is Whiteheadian deism.

Regarding God's availability for prehension by finite occasions, it might be argued that, although the divine concrescence is not finally complete at any time, it is complete enough to be hybrid-physically prehended. Any phase of God would in fact be complete or satisfied with respect to the perfect response God makes to the yet antecedent state of the world in light of the primordial nature. The lack of completeness would stem from the fact that God has not yet responded to future states of the world; the divine concrescence must be everlasting because God must keep up with an everlasting world.

The question must be asked, however, whether in this interpretation the incompleteness of God's finite phases results from partiality of subjective form. Admittedly, God can alter the subjective form of a given phase's prehension by grading it up or down in some subsequent phase; in the nineteenth century, for instance, God probably thought the Congress of Vienna more important than the American settling of the Oregon Territory, but would probably reverse that valuation today. But the question is whether in the earlier phase God was completely determinate in the divine judgment for that phase, or whether God was partially indeterminate awaiting further events. If the former, then, it would seem that a physical prehension of that phase by a finite occasion is possible; but there would be no reason in that phase for further concrescence. As far as Divinity is concerned, at that point God is satisfied, completely determinate. Only an external input from a later phase of the world could rouse God to a new phase of concrescence. If the latter, then the continuity of God's everlasting concrescence is insured but at the cost of the prehendability of any finite divine phase: The very thing a finite occasion's hybrid physical prehension is supposed to grasp of God is his conceptual valuation, which on this horn of the dilemma is partially incomplete at any finite phase.

Suppose, however, that we let this interpretation of the incompleteness of the phases of God's everlasting concrescence pass without question. What about the other kind of isolation, namely, the divine inability to prehend the world because God has no initial phase after any finite state of the world? The line of objection to this point would be to point out the difference between God and finite occasions. Both are actual entities. But a finite occasion begins with initial physical data, supplements this with conceptual prehensions, including novel ones, and reaches satisfaction with a new physical reality. God by contrast begins concrescence with the eternal primordial nature as initial datum, supplements this with prehensions of the physical world and, in each phase, reaches at least partial satisfaction (depending on the interpretation of the argument in the previous paragraph) in the form of a conceptual appreciation of the value of the world and the divine nature. Given this contrast, more or less clear in Whitehead, it is unfair to interpret God's concrescence according to the same categories of explanation and obligation used for finite occasions. We must be allowed to say, for instance, that whereas all supplemental appearances for finite occasions derive by conceptual valuation, reversion or transmutation from the initial data, all supplementation for God derives from divine prehension of the latest occasions of the finite world. Whereas finite occasions arise from what is not themselves, enter into subjective immediacy in becoming themselves and emerge into public fact for later occasions, God's everlasting concrescence begins in the immediacy of the primordial nature, grows by supplementation from the external world and returns to the immediacy of God's subjective appreciation.

This line of objection certainly is plausible. Whitehead said so little about God that any comprehensive theory of God's concrescence must be yet invented.[12] His remarks about God's having to *exhibit* as well as establish the categoreal scheme perhaps have been interpreted too enthusiastically. The point, however, is that this conception of God is so alien to that of a finite actual occasion that the doctrine of genetic successiveness simply cannot be transferred from one to another.

The argument made before regarding the sense in which God's finite phases are complete illustrates the impossibility of transferring the conception of genetic successiveness from finite occasions to God. For finite occasions, incompleteness consists in a lack of complete integration in subjective form, not in the possibility the subjective form be changed in a later phase. Yet, if this is true of God, then God cannot be prehended. Suppose we say that, due to infinite conceptuality, God can completely integrate any finite phase; in this case reintegration depends on supplementation from the finite world. But whence is the continuity in the genetic successiveness? Not in any need that an early phase has for further determination. But it is part of the doctrine of genetic successiveness that the continuity of concrescence is in the continuity of the subjective aim needing further phases of modification to attain complete determination! For God, the continuity can only consist in infinite conceptuality, which is continuous only because it is primordial to the finite phases of God's everlasting concrescence.

Of the two sides of my claim that God is isolated if interpreted as having an everlasting genetically temporal concrescence, the one saying God is never determinate enough to be finitely prehended is fairly well established. The side saying God cannot prehend the world may indeed be adequately rebutted by showing God's concrescence is very unlike a finite occasion's. But this latter move jeopardizes the interpretive force of claiming God's concrescence is a genetically temporal concrescence; the meaning of the genetic process derives precisely from the categories of explanation and obligation defining finite concrescence.

I have avoided saying that Ford moves from his analysis of genetic successiveness to the claim that God's concrescence is genetically temporal. He says, in fact, in "The Non-temporality of Whitehead's God," that God's concrescence is nontemporal, combining the nontemporality of the primordial nature with the temporality of the consequent nature. Yet he also in that essay recognizes the force of the argument that God must have attained satisfaction to be prehended by a finite occasion, and argues himself that God is satisfied, by virtue of infinite conceptuality, at every moment. I take this to be a strong suggestion that God's concrescence is supposed to be genetically temporal; it is nontemporal only in the physical sense of temporality.

But then my argument returns yet again. If God is satisfied at every phase, is not God *physically* temporal? Genetic temporality is supposed to be supersession of less satisfied phases by more nearly satisfied ones. Whether or not Ford himself goes so far as to assert that God's concrescence is genetically temporal, he tends in that direction and it is an interesting one to follow. But it is difficult to see how this position has found solid ground between the isolation of a self-defining genetic concrescence and the very plain temporality of Hartshorne's social God.

III

There are many attractive reasons for admitting Ford's point that genetic division reveals a dynamic process of decision, not merely a set of patterns of increasing complexity of integration. The point about decision can be accepted by itself, emphasizing the genetic process as the coming-to-be of occasions rather than as a set of existent phases, and limiting its application to finite actual occasions. For the point cannot be applied to God. By admitting this limitation, however, are we left without a clue as to the nature of God?

I believe not. We could always move to the Hartshornean conception of God as a society of divine occasions: God is here conceived as present in each divine occasion prehending the absolute supremacy of the previous divine occasion without loss, and also prehending the contingencies of the world as it unfolds in time. There are two related and unfortunate consequences of this conception, however, that can be mentioned here prior to an elaborate discussion in Chapter Four. Because each divine occasion prehends the absolute and necessary metaphysical nature of divinity in a previous divine occasion, God is always and everywhere subject to the strictures of necessity. Hartshorne's interpretation of the ontological argument reinforces this. But most theistic religious traditions suggest that God, in at least some respects, transcends the limits of necessity and perhaps creates them. Whitehead was closer to experience, I shall argue subsequently, in saying the primordial nature both establishes the categoreal conditions and, being infinite, cannot be exhausted in finite phases of response to the world.[13] Furthermore, if God is limited to the society of divine experiences—of the world and of divine occasions—the contingent and relative occasions must contain the universal principles of necessity exhaustively within themselves; Hartshorne insists that the necessary side of God is the abstract pole of the divine dipolar nature. Yet it is difficult to see how a universal can be exhausted in even an infinite set of instantiations. It seems preferable to say with Whitehead that God's primordial created fact, the primordial conceptual valuation, is eternal and in itself nonrelative to temporal occasions. Is there an alternative between Ford's divine genetic successiveness and Hartshorne's divine sociality?

Suppose we say, as suggested in the previous chapter, that God is creator, *ex nihilo,* of every finite determination. God could create, in every occasion, the novel determinations of the subjective aim, in both the initial and subsequent phases; or better, God could create each occasion by contributing the novel determinations of its phases of coming to be. Because the objective determinations in an occasion, deriving from its prehension of the past, themselves were occasions integrating objective data with novel subjective form, God is creator of all determinations by creating determinations of subjective form, either in the present or in the past relative to any moment.[14] Because novel determinations of subjective form enter an occasion not by the occasion's prehending God, but by God's creating them there, no need exists to show that God is determinate enough in a finite time to be prehended. If God is known, it is through creating revelations of the divine creative character; God at least can be known as creator of this particular world.[15] Because God is not separate from the creative act, God is not separate from the creatures so as to have a problem knowing them. Furthermore, the creator does not have to prehend only the objective character of occasions as finished facts; as creator, God is at the heart of their coming-to-be.[16] To say God is creator in this strong sense preserves the transcendence Ford seeks in emphasizing the primordial nature in Whitehead's concept; but it avoids the isolation of God from the world resulting from interpreting the divine life as a genetically temporal concrescence.

To review our argument so far, we may recall that in the first chapter we noted that Whitehead's decisive innovation in the contemporary context of philosophical theology has been to distinguish God from creativity. In developing this point, we have followed the line of interpretation pursued most imaginatively by Lewis S. Ford. If God is distinct from creativity, and subject to it (as Whitehead claims), then the structures of process involved in creativity must apply somehow to God. In the hypothesis that God is a single actual entity, the genetic process within the divine concrescence may very well account for God's coming to completely definite satisfaction, but only at the price of being unable to prehend the world at any finite time, and of being too indefinite to be prehended by a worldly occasion at any finite time. Chapters Four and Five shall consider the hypothesis that God is a society of occasions each of which is temporally located and capable of relating to ordinary finite occasions.

But before abandoning the line of interpretation developed by Ford, it is necessary to examine the wisdom of distinguishing God from creativity from yet another angle. Let us suppose that there were no problems with the conception of God, so distinguished. What about the conception of creativity?

One of the traditional reasons for connecting God and creativity has been to address the problem of the one and the many. How are the many things in the world diverse on the one hand and related on the other? The traditional answer is by being created by God. Can creativity distinct from God, as Whitehead distinguished them, solve the problem of the one and the many?

· III ·

Ontology of the
One and the Many

Whitehead's distinctive contribution to the discussion of
the one and the many was to assign the unifying functions traditionally ascribed to God to two different factors. On
the one hand, the actual unifying of the world, the bringing of
potential diversity into actual harmony, he assigned to concrete
actual entities; among the actual entities is God, the rest being
temporal occasions.[1] The actual unity of concrete facts is a function of the interaction between God and the world as described in
Part V of *Process and Reality*, part of which was quoted earlier in
Chapter One. On the other hand, ontological creation, the unification of one and many that makes actual entities possible, was
assigned to the principle of creativity in the category of the ultimate.

The importance of this strategy is that it underscores a distinction between two basic senses of cause, corresponding respec-
tively with two basic senses of unity that must be accounted for
in a solution to the problem of the one and the many. One sense
of cause is associated with the ontological principle; the other
with the category of the ultimate, especially creativity. Corresponding to these, the kind of unity accounted for by the causes
associated with the ontological principle may be called cosmological; the kind accounted for by the category of the ultimate may be
called ontological. The burden of this chapter, however, is that
the category of the ultimate as developed by Whitehead is *not*
sufficient to account for ontological unity.

I

The explanation of the distinctions between the different senses of cause and the different senses of unity will lay the groundwork for the argument against Whitehead.

1. The ontological principle is that any condition in any particular instance in the process of becoming is to be accounted for either in terms of the decision of some antecedent in its actual world, or in the decision of its own concrescence.[2] Reference to the former kind of decision is a matter of efficient causation, to the latter of final causation. All decisions are made in the subjective immediacy of some actual entity's experience. They involve establishing the selective emphasis of each of the data given in the initial phase of the subjective experience so that in the final objectification the experience is completely determinate.[3] Decisions are made in accordance with the subjective aim of the experient occasions, but the subjective aim is itself subject to modification throughout the phases of the process.[4] The modification of the decisive subjective aim consists in a reaction of the experient whole on itself; in this sense, each occasion gives itself its own reasons for its decisions.[5]

The kind of *causation* associated with the ontological principle, therefore, is a matter of decision and of the objective results of prior decisions. The ontological principle says that for every particular factor there is a decision somewhere that accounts for it; the corresponding kind of causal analysis involves hunting for the occasions that through their own self-creativity determine the factor to exist. Whitehead reformulated the ontological principle in many ways to say that nothing enters the universe that is not the product of some actual entity's decision.

The *unity* pointed to by the ontological principle is of many determinate states of the cosmos, that is, satisfactions of actual entities. The ontological principle directs the examination of any particular actual entity. And it directs the examination of the cosmos as a whole, referring to decisions in temporal actual occasions and in God's primordial and consequent natures. The primordial valuation of eternal objects is referred to God's primordial decision. The determinate satisfactions of temporal actual occasions are referred to the occasions' own decisions, to the other occasions prehended in the experience and to the hybrid-physical prehension of God's primordial valuation constituting the initial subjective aim. The satisfaction of God's experience of the world at any time is referred in its various parts to the divine primordial valuation, to the decisions of the actual occasions in the world, to God's previous consequent decisions and to God's immediate decision. In turn, God's decisive experience of the world enters the experience of subsequent temporal occasions and must be referred to as a kind of reason in their satisfaction. The ontological principle accounts for the unity of any plurality that enters into the constitution of an actual entity; anywhere there is a standpoint at which a plurality is unified, the ontological principle says there are decisions—either in the world of the standpoint or in the standpoint itself—that account for the unity. This is the kind of unity, a unity of actual entities and ingressed eternal objects, that can be called a *cosmological* unity.

The kind of question the ontological principle interprets is how this or that ingression of eternal objects occurred, or how this or that objectification of an actual entity or nexus occurred. It does *not* answer the question why there is any decision at all, why any eternal objects ingress, why there is any objectification of actual entities, or why there are any actual entities. Yet these latter are the questions generally associated with ontology. In Whitehead's scheme, not the ontological principle, but the category of the ultimate addresses these questions. The ontological principle is misleadingly named. It should be called the *cosmological* principle, since it deals with the constitution of the particularities of this cosmos.

2. The ontological question as to why there exist any cosmological unities is answered, allegedly, by the category of the ultimate. One, many and creativity are the notions making up the category. They are probably what Whitehead had foremost in mind when he characterized the coherence of notions not as the defining of each in terms of the others, but as the presupposing of each by the others "so that in isolation they are meaningless." Coherence means "that what is indefinable in one such notion cannot be abstracted from its relevance to the other notions."[6] One, many and creativity cannot be defined either by themselves or in terms of each other, but what is indefinable in each one is relevant

to the others. One, according to Whitehead, "stands for the singularity of an entity" and, although singularity cannot be defined as such, it presupposes the notion of *many* singulars in "disjunctive diversity."[7] Disjunctive diversity, of course, presupposes many singulars.

Most philosophers would take the system of mutual presupposition on the level of the problem of the one and the many to consist in those two notions, one and many. The heart of Whitehead's philosophy is that creativity is presupposed on the same level, as it were, and in turn presupposes one and many.

> The ultimate metaphysical principle is the advance from disjunction to conjunction, creating a novel entity other than the entities given in disjunction. The novel entity is at once the togetherness of the "many" which it finds, and also it is one among the disjunctive "many" which it leaves.... The many become one and are increased by one. In their natures, entities are disjunctively "many" in process of passage into conjunctive unity.[8]

It is inconceivable that there be a many or a one except that one is conceived as a unification of many, and many is conceived as a disjunction of such unifications of manys. The process of unifying many into one is creativity; the process is creative since, when the many is unified into one, there is one more singular than when the many is not unified.

The kind of *causation* associated with the category of the ultimate is ontological. It answers the question, "Why does there exist a unification of that manifold of actual entities?" The answer is, "Where there is a many, creativity creates a one unifying them." This differs from the cosmological causation associated with the ontological principle; there the relevant question is, "Why is this satisfaction as it is?" The cosmological answer is, "Because of these decisions in its own coming-to-be and those decisions in its actual world." The cosmological inquiry is epistemologically independent of the ontological account of why there is a satisfaction given to inquire about.

The kind of *unity* associated with the category of the ultimate is correspondingly ontological. Whereas cosmological unity is a matter of objective unification of actual entities in the satisfaction

of another actual entity, ontological unity is the primordial togetherness of actual entities necessary for prehension and articulated by the creativity binding many into one. The category of
the ultimate described the condition for the existence of any actual entity. There could be no harmonious satisfaction, expressive
of the ontological principle, were there not the basic relation of
ones and manys through creativity. If there were no creativity,
the many would individually perish without objective trace, and
no one unifying them would be possible; of course, they in turn
would have been impossible.

3. In summary, Whitehead separated the functions of creative
unification usually ascribed to God, giving the ontological functions to the category of the ultimate and the cosmological functions to actual entities' decisions according to the ontological
principle. This reflects, in reverse order, the distinction between
cosmological causation and unities with which the ontological
principle is associated and ontological causes and unities with
which the category of the ultimate, especially creativity, is associated. Whitehead's characteristic emphasis on the freedom of
every actual entity to be self-creative in relative independence
from every other actual entity, including God, rests on this separation. In the more usual view of creative unification, God in
some sense is the source of both ontological and cosmological
unity, with created entities being the cause of the latter in some
different but complementary sense. But, along with the more
usual view, goes a commitment to the thesis that God is intimately present as creator to every creature even in the subjectivity of the creature's free self-constitution. In the usual view people are not free from God's creativity, whereas in Whitehead's
view God's creative influence is limited to the provision of data
for the finite actual occasions to objectify, as discussed in the previous chapter.

II

The separation of the functions of creative unity depends on
the category of the ultimate to give an adequate account of ontological unity. There is good reason to think its account is inadequate; this section will examine the reason.

Creativity is the principle that every plurality of actual entities is creatively unified into a new actual entity. But there is a problem here; in what sense is creativity a "principle"? It might be an empirical generalization, stating that in fact all pluralities get creatively unified; but this would fail to account for the ontological problem of *why* they get unified. Or creativity might be interpreted as a principle in a more normative sense, to the effect that pluralities *must* get unified; but Whitehead's theory precludes this interpretation. These two interpretive hypotheses will be elaborated in turn.

1. Consider the alternative that the notion of creativity merely generalizes the descriptive facts of how every occasion is a creative unification of initial data. This is an inadequate ontological account, it seems to me, because it does not give a reason for why there exist any events of creative unification. In effect it fails to advance ontologically beyond the ontological principle, which, *taking for granted the creative unification*, accounts for the specific form of the unification in terms of decisions. The ontological principle by itself is sufficient to acknowledge that the events of creative unification take place and, if the category of the ultimate is merely an empirical generalization, then it is not necessary at all. With it or without it, the ontological question is begged.

2. Consider then that the category of the ultimate might be a normative principle determining that there must be creative unifications of manys. Whitehead was clear, however, that creativity is indeterminate in abstraction from concrete events that exhibit it.[9] As the universal of universals, creativity is grasped by intuition in specific occasions and has no character apart from them that may be described. The actual creativity of any occasion is a matter of the decisions making it up. But then if creativity apart from specific occasions is completely indeterminate, it cannot be normative in any sense that would necessitate creativity in specific occasions.

Two rebuttals of this objection are to be expected.

First, it might be said that the sense in which Whitehead meant creativity to be indeterminate is solely a matter of the problems of conception and not a matter of complete lack of character in creativity itself. After all, the reason creativity cannot be described is that any description must be more special than it, and hence distorting; Whitehead intended for there to be content to the intuition of creativity over and above the cosmological character of the specific entities in which it is embodied.

The difficulty with this rebuttal, however, is that the determinate character needed for creativity is one constitutive of a necessity for creative unification in entities; this necessity must be contrastable with the contingency that there be no creative unification (even if the latter is self-contradictory) and such a contrast would indeed by describable, at least as a contrast. But then it could not be a matter of intuition, and creativity could not be the universal of universals; rather, the ground of the contrast would be the universal of universals. To respond to the basic ontological problem, the category of the ultimate would have to show why there is creativity instead of nothing.

The second rebuttal is that creativity *by itself* need not be normative for specific occasions. Rather, it is normative only *relative* to specific occasions, and the relevance is contributed by God in his primordial nature.[10] God can be said to determine not only the relevance of eternal objects as possibilities for the unification, but also the necessity that there be a creative event unifying. The difficulty here, however, is the self-referential one. Creativity is required to explain why there is any creative actuality, even the creation of the primordial created fact of relevance. It cannot be that God creates the normative relevance of the category of the ultimate *according to the category of the ultimate.* There would be no normative relevance of the category *for that primordial creative act.* That act would be an exception to the category; it would illustrate it, and this would allow it not to be an exception if the category were only an empirical generalization. But if the category is normative, the primordial divine creative act is an exception to its obligatoriness. Put another way, the unification of actual entities with the category of the ultimate which might be normative for them must be the product of some decision, as required by the ontological principle; but the reason for there being any decision at all is what the category of the ultimate is supposed to explain.

3. The conclusion to draw is that the category of the ultimate does not genuinely address the ontological question, but only records the ontological situation, namely, that there are actual entities whose being consists in constituting themselves as unifica-

tions of manys. In effect, the category of the ultimate is only an empirical generalization. This accords with Whitehead's description of cosmology as imaginative generalization in the first chapter of *Process and Reality* and with his specific application of this interpretation of philosophy to creativity.[11]

III

But what conclusions, then, can we draw about Whitehead's contribution to the discussion of the one and the many? We might simply note that he would reject the ontological question. He would claim it is just impossible to say why there are real things, why there are creative actual entities.[12] But is he entitled to stop there?

1. The basic ontological problem is to account for the unity of many and one through creativity. The category of the ultimate is a statement of the ontological problem, not the answer to it. The ontological unity is *de facto*, not *de jure*. Every actual entity is an instance of ontological unity as well as an enjoyment of its specific cosmological unity; it is a unification through creativity of its initial data as such into an objective satisfaction as such, as well as a unification of the specific characters of its initial data into the specific character of its satisfaction. According to the ontological principle, there ought to be somewhere a creative decision responsible for any unification. But the decisions of all actual entities, precisely because they are creative, cannot constitute the ontological unity as the condition for creativity. There could be no creative actual entities if there were no unity of one and many through creativity. Not even the divine primordial decision could constitute this ontological unity in God's own creativity or in others' creativity, since that decision, being creative, depends on a prior ontological unity of many and one in creativity. Therefore, *given the ontological principle*, with no possibility of an ontological decision, the ontological unity of many and one in creativity is impossible! Any attempt to exempt the category of the ultimate from criticism at this point is only special pleading. Whitehead is not entitled to reject the ontological question.

2. Whitehead's response here, then, would have to be that the ontological principle does not apply to ontological unity in the sense

described. There is no decision responsible for the basic togetherness of one and many in creativity. Precisely because the category
of the ultimate is the universal of universals there can be nothing
"responsible" for it. Creativity must simply be accepted as something given.

The issue here is whether the irrationality of the category of
the ultimate must be accepted. Whitehead was right to see that
any complex unity is contingent and needs an account. The cosmological unities of actual satisfactions are contingent upon and
accounted for by actual decisions; but that kind of account cannot
suffice for ontological unity. Ontological unity is a contingent
complexity in its own way, a complex of one and many in creative
process. Of course, neither ones nor manys nor creativity could
exist except as together; but the question is why they exist at all.
If Whitehead accepts the irrationality of the category of the ultimate, he accepts an irrationality in one place yet does not accept it
in an analogous one; he might as well say that events happen with
pure spontaneity and no causation.

We rightly boggle at this. It is a betrayal of rational faith.[13]

3. The criticism of Whitehead made here would be only a
complaint about inelegance in his theory if it went no farther than
it has. It might simply be the case that no account of ontological
unity as exhibited in the category of the ultimate can be given.
This seems not to be the case, however. Another account is possible, and it rests on a different construction of the primitive notion of creativity.

Whitehead took creativity to be the bringing about of a one
that unifies a many through its own creative self-constitution.
This may in fact be descriptive of the cosmological process; but it
cannot be descriptive of the grounding of the ontological unity.

The alternate conception is that creativity is the bringing about
of a many in an act that itself constitutes the creative source to be
a unified agent, a one for the created product. The creative source
is admittedly indeterminate apart from any connection with creation. But in the act of creation, the source constitutes itself as
creator and as one relative to many. This kind of creativity does
not presuppose an ontological unity because it is not a reduction
of a multiplicity to unity through a novel entity, nor a production
of a multiplicity out of a unity. It is the creation of both unity and

multiplicity *ex nihilo*, the creation of determinateness as such.

4. The latter conception of creativity legitimately can be called ontological creativity because it can account for ontological unity. Whitehead's conception of creativity cannot account for ontological unity because it is defined on a par with one and many. The alternate conception is that one and many are both the products of the creative act, along with the cosmological creativity that relates them (if Whitehead's description of process is correct). The very interrelation of one, many and cosmological creativity that makes Whitehead's category of the ultimate irrational indicates that the notions and what they signify are contingent upon ontological creativity.

Since ontological creativity is productive of all determinate plurality, including its own character, it cannot proceed according to any preestablished principles. In this sense, then, there is no explanation of why this world is created that has process in it rather than one without process. Whitehead was correct that philosophy must accept concrete fact and explain the abstractions of it; at root philosophy is empirical, and its object is the world that happens to be one of process. But the advance made by appealing to ontological creativity is that it can be explained how such a world is possible; it is ontologically created, not by decisions within its own process—that would be self-referentially absurd—but by a transcendent creator that makes itself creator in the act of creating. Although this advance does not give a reason why there is this world rather than that, it gives a reason how there could be any world.

5. Whitehead's system must be reassessed if the idea of ontological creativity is valid over and above the cosmological creativity in the category of the ultimate. Two points of reassessment can be mentioned.

First, the distinction should be drawn and clearly maintained between ontological and cosmological creativity. As noncompeting notions, every actual entity would have to exhibit both kinds. Each entity would be both (a) cosmologically creative in its own right and (b) the product, together with the entities it prehends and that prehend it, of ontological creation. In some respects the recognition of ontological creativity is merely complementary to Whitehead's system as it stands. In other respects at least rhetorical qualifications may have to be introduced; for instance, regarding freedom, actual entities would be self-creative only in the cosmological sense—in the ontological sense they would be wholly dependent.

Second, Whitehead's conception of God as an actual entity functioning relative to the world in the cosmological ways described in Part V of *Process and Reality* and quoted earlier in Chapter One must be compared to the conception of the ontological creator constituting itself the creator of the world by creating it. Certainly the latter is closer than Whitehead's conception to what the Western tradition has regarded as the God of religion. If Whitehead's theory in fact requires the recognition of an ontological creator as well as an infinite actual entity, then the question as to which should be called God must be reopened.

Of course, if there are such difficulties as were alleged in the previous chapter with Whitehead's concept of God as an actual entity, then perhaps that conception should be dropped altogether in favor of that of the ontological creator.[14]

IV

A profound metaphysical issue underlies the discussion of this chapter. It concerns the nature of an ultimately satisfying explanation. There are two broad sensibilities regarding this which are so diverse as to be virtually impossible to mediate.

On the one hand is the view that an ultimately satisfying explanation is a reduction of things to first principles. Things are explained by being shown to exhibit characters necessitated by certain determinate first principles. The first principles explain by virtue of their own character. If it is asked how the first principles themselves are to be accounted for, the answer is that they do not need to be accounted for if indeed they are "first"—the ultimate and primordial explanatory principles. The Hartshornean line of philosophical theology is clearly within this rationalist sensibility. Whitehead's treatment of the category of the ultimate, if it is accurately analyzed as an empirical generalization, is also of this sort.

On the other hand, there is the empiricist's view that an ultimately satisfying explanation consists in locating the decisive actions from which things take their form. To be satisfied is to see the loci of decisive determination. A theory of an ontological creator surely falls within this sensibility regarding explanation, for it claims that even the first principles, being determinate, need an account, and the only thing that could account for them is an ontologically creative act.[15] Whitehead's ontological principle, emphasizing that actual entities are to be accounted for by reference to decisions in various actual entities, accords with this sensibility on the cosmological level. But Whitehead does not apply the reference to decision to the ontological level, and thereby slips into rationalism. Or at least Whitehead opened the door to addressing the ontological question in a rationalist way, even though he did not do that himself.

The difficulty alleged against the empiricist sensibility is that there is nothing in the character of the ontologically creative act that accounts for the product of the act (as indeed there cannot be if everything determinate must be within the product); therefore, explanation by reference to a decisive action is not an explanation at all, but merely a pointing at what needs explanation. But then, this objection begs the question in favor of the rationalist sensibility, since only a rationalist would want something determinate in the *character* of the explanatory principle that would explain. Being of the empiricist sort, I can only confess that the rationalist approach cannot account for existence, for the ontological issues, because it must presuppose the normative existence of the explanatory first principles. Only the empiricist approach can address the problem of accounting for the reality of things. If philosophical theology is to account for the reality of things, then it should have a bias toward the empiricist sensibility. Surely the existential quality of religious experience is empiricistic in this sense!

If the empiricist sensibility cannot be "proved," perhaps it can at least make itself dialectically persuasive through considering the alternative. Within the tradition of process theology, the systematic views of Charles Hartshorne substantially represent the rationalist perspective. The next step in my argument, therefore, must be a fairly comprehensive review and analysis of his position.

·IV·

God as Social

I

Although Charles Hartshorne clearly is a process philosopher and theologian in Whitehead's tradition, he has also developed a systematic philosophic position in his own right. In part, his divergences from Whitehead result from what he perceives to be ambiguities or weaknesses internal to Whitehead's view. But, more interestingly, they stem from his consideration of the place of process thinking in the history of philosophy.

Two things stand out in Hartshorne's reading of history, as expressed for instance in his systematic work, *Creative Synthesis and Philosophic Method.*[1] First, his philosophy finds a location in the history of philosophy only by reinterpreting the main emphasis of that history. In a sense every new philosophical position requires a reinterpretation of history. Whitehead had attempted something of the sort in Part II of *Process and Reality.* But Hartshorne carries the reinterpretation out rather thoroughly, from Plato and Aristotle to Nagel, Quine, Wittgenstein and von Wright.

Second, Hartshorne takes the history of philosophy to include Indian and Chinese philosophy as well as the footnoters to Plato. Not since Hegel has a major philosopher had this catholicity, and Hegel ruined his point by relating the traditions sequentially, not as alternatives. What allows Hartshorne to take the other traditions seriously? The answer must be in his reinterpretation of history itself. Like Whitehead, he attacks the idea of substance as supposed by the Western tradition since the Greeks. In the West this attack seems preposterous. But in India and China, only an aberrant mind would believe in enduring substances! As Hartshorne points out, the age in which a responsible thinker can be ignorant of the traditions of the East is past.

Furthermore, as a process philosopher Hartshorne is entirely persuasive, at least to me, on at least seven basic points that condition the problem of God.

Hartshorne has not only argued for but demonstrated by example the importance of metaphysics. In his context, metaphysics means the study of the conditions for, or what would be true in, any possible world. His view does not imply that possibilities apply wholesale to "worlds," or that an alternative to the present state of affairs is a whole "other world," but only that whatever is possible must illustrate metaphysical principles. Hartshorne calls metaphysical statements a priori, and there may be some problems about that (discussed on page 70ff.); but it is clear that metaphysical statements are not subject to test in any ordinary experiential way. Their importance lies in this, that the metaphysical structure of the world sets the conditions for experience and, if that structure is misunderstood, experience itself will be misunderstood. One cannot do without metaphysics; one can only have a better or worse metaphysics. Hartshorne amply demonstrates the implications of metaphysics not only for religion, but also for science, for morals and for the encounter of world cultures.

He demonstrates further the importance of systematic philosophy. Not all metaphysics is systematic and not only metaphysics is systematic. In fact, Hartshorne's preoccupation with apriori philosophy may have led him to neglect a systematic consideration of some of the more experiential elements of life. But he shows the importance of system in another way. In discussing why proofs for the existence of God are valuable, in light of the fact people might still reject the premises, Hartshorne points out that, at the very least, the proofs illuminate the price of rejecting the conclusion: namely, having to reject some of the premises or habits of inference.[2] So it is with the systematic connections of all life—to reject some belief in one domain might require paying a price somewhere else. The pedestrian applicability of this point is obvious in this day of environmental collapse beneath the weight of technological exploitation.

Hartshorne shows as well the viability of construing *creativity* rather than *being* as the basic metaphysical category. Whitehead, of course, had elaborated a system in which *being* was defined as *potentiality for becoming in the creative process,* and Bergson earlier had argued that someone ought to invent such a system. But Hartshorne shows the viability of this program by using the Whiteheadian categories to sort through the main problems and figures of philosophy. Whereas it could still have been argued against Whitehead that creativity is basic *only within his own system,* a bizarre and noologistic system at that, Hartshorne has shown that a great many other philosophers would have been better off with creativity at the root of *their* vision. But "viability" is a weasel word for describing a philosophy. Earlier, in Chapter Three, I argued that Whitehead's notion of creativity answers only some cosmological questions about the world, leaving the more ultimate ontological ones untouched. For his part, Hartshorne's interpretation of God so qualifies his meaning of creativity that the contrast between becoming and eternity within the cosmological process is softened, reduced in fact to what Peirce would call a "degenerate third."[3] So I must claim that Hartshorne ultimately is at two removes from the truth. What was proposed above as true is that the important category at the ontological level has to do with creation *ex nihilo,* not with creativity bringing a new "one" out of antecedent manifolds. And at the cosmological level something like Plato's irreducible contrast between *being* and *becoming* exhibits more intensity for experience than the swallowing of being in becoming, or vice versa.

Hartshorne masterfully demonstrates the importance of memory and perception for causation, and shows how Whitehead's notion of "prehension" is a brilliant example of metaphysical generalization.[4] One thing causes another by being prehended by it, and prehension is of some past occasion of experience. Hartshorne goes a long way toward showing the viability of this notion for interpreting causation in general, but he does not show how the theory of prehension can render a consistent *theory* of causation (something Whitehead did in *Process and Reality*). Rather, Hartshorne shows how the idea of prehension (he does not often use the technical term, preferring instead experiential terms like perception and memory) handles issues as formulated by the public philosophical discussion. This advance from the privacy of Whitehead's system to the public arena is one of Hartshorne's most important contributions.

The qualification I would append to the viability Hartshorne demonstrates for prehension is to restore the doctrine of "perishing"to the significance Whitehead gave it. Hartshorne is concerned to say that actualities do not perish in any significant sense.

> Whitehead calls all past events "actual entities," or "actual occasions," and this in spite of his saying that actualities "perish," a metaphor which has sadly misled many (unless something else has sadly misled me). They "perish yet live for evermore" is the final word of *Process and Reality,* and to this I adhere, whether or not Whitehead did. The perishing, taken anything like literally, is an illusion occasioned by the hiddenness of deity from us. But, as Whitehead at least sometimes explicates the term, it has nothing to do with an internal change from vital actuality to a corpse or skeleton, but is merely the fact that the definite actual subject is now *also* object for further subjects. No longer is it the latest verge of actuality, since there is now a richer reality, including the once latest one. This has nothing to do, at least in my theory, with an inner shrinkage or impoverishment.[5]

Significant or not, there is something lost from the present becoming of an occasion when it has finished becoming and is past. The occasion has lost its *subjective feeling of being in process.* This feeling has to do with entertaining a somewhat vague proposition as a lure for one's own concretion, with subjective elements of negativity in not having embodied that proposition, in having alternative concretions, and so forth. To be sure, there are propositions intermediate in the concrescence of an occasion expressing this feeling of being in process. All prehension of past conscious thought depends upon a subsequent occasion's having a hybrid-physical prehension of these intermediate propositions as embodied in the objectified subjective form of the finished occasion. In this sense, all continuity of conscious life depends on the objectification of those intermediate propositions. But there is a difference between such propositions themselves and the subjective feeling of them. Those propositions are enjoyed subjectively, and that gives them the special tone of subjective life. The feeling of deciding is not the same as entertaining in propositional form the alternatives for decision. Subjective life is the feeling of incompleteness on the way to completion. It is the feeling of self-creativity. And *that* must pass away when completion is attained.

Is the perishing of subjective immediacy of creativity in an occasion a matter of significance? It seems to me this issue depends on whether one's ultimate ontology is a monism in which the world is summed up in its achieved value—a value-oriented twist on the Aristotelian notion that the best being is that which is complete in itself—or a fundamental dualism in which value-achievement is always contrasted with creative value-achieving. Hartshorne holds to the former view, whereas Whitehead held to the latter. The point here is that the loss of immediacy of becoming is of essential significance to the dualistic view. If becoming stands in fundamental ontological contrast with being, then the rhythm of creating *and perishing* must be integrated with the rhythm of a many which becomes a one (which in turn is part of a new many which becomes a new one, and so forth). Of course the rhythm of the immediate process has no being or achievement other than the determinate occasions it brings to fact; but that is the poignancy of change and becoming, always losing its thrust when it succeeds. And I must admit that Whitehead, in his discussion of the category of the Ultimate in *Process and Reality,* emphasized the accomplishment in reality of the definite manys and ones, to the subordination of the infinite incompletion of creativity. Nevertheless, if we say, as I think we should, that the subjective feeling of creative unification of the incomplete is at the heart of human experience and the universe, and that our ontology should reflect this by maintaining the fundamental contrast between creative becoming and accomplished being, then perishing is a very important doctrine indeed!

Hartshorne presents an effective case against determinism; this is the fifth item about which I find him significantly persuasive. In his introduction to *Creative Synthesis and Philosophic Method,* he develops the notion of creativity through a careful polemic against determinism, and argues persuasively that no event can be analyzed exhaustively into the realities of its antecedents. At the very least the event must synthesize the antecedents into its own self. Even if the pattern for synthesis comes from antecedents, the synthesizing itself is new. It is interesting to complement Hartshorne's arguments in this regard with Paul Weiss's. Weiss's usual line is to say that, if determinism is true, no change can take place because there could be nothing new.[6] Hartshorne and Weiss are not usually so nicely complementary.

Hartshorne furthermore has demonstrated the viability of the doctrine that *events*, not substances, are the basic individuals of the world. Again, the theory was Whitehead's, at least in its rough contours, but the viability for public discussion comes from Hartshorne's work. The main defense of the doctrine of substance has been that it is required to make sense of predication, and Hartshorne attacks this belief at its core. This is the point at which he cites the authority of the Buddhist tradition with good results. The Buddhists, of course, have never been taken in by the substance doctrine, and Hartshorne reminds us we do not have to grope back to a few epigrams from Heraclitus to get a considerable body of interpretation of the claim that all things flow.[7]

Perhaps, however, Hartshorne has not proved as much as he would like. His chief polemical focus is to show that individual events are the most concrete of things because the connectives between events, taken by themselves, are always somewhat abstract and indifferent to the adventitious determinations of the events connected. True enough. But the question has long been raised, by Weiss among others, whether this view of events, and of persons as event sequences, properly accounts for the continuity of the enduring human being.[8] At the outset it can be admitted that the continuity is perhaps not as concrete as the events themselves. But for most human purposes the continuity is much more important than the concreteness, and although Hartshorne admits this, he does not see much force in the point.[9]

As a final point of persuasiveness, Hartshorne has made the case for the greater excellence of relativity over independence. Just as he rejects the substance doctrine of ultimate individuals, so he rejects the correlative belief, stemming from Aristotle, that self-sufficiency, the ability to be complete by oneself, is the greatest kind of excellence. Rather, the greater excellence is in being sensitive and responsive to the elements in the environment.[10]

The process model of a thing, of course, is the self-constitution of a new entity out of a plurality of past things, and Whitehead had worked out the basic logic of this position. But Hartshorne shows its advantages in a range of questions from metaphysics on the one side to ethics on the other. To be *un*related to something existent in one's environment, to which there is a real possibility of being related, is a mark of stupidity and fragility.

Philosophical theses can have plausibility (or implausibility) on at least two levels. On the first, they can be defended individually in the dialectic of the public discussion. On the second, they can be defended as interpreted by a comprehensive systematic metaphysical theory. On the first level, the interpretive theory is presupposed but employed vaguely, or suppressed from the discussion entirely. On the second level, the individual theses stand or fall with the whole theory interpreting them. Hartshorne has successfully defended the points made in this section mainly on the first level. In consonance with the present critique of process theology, I have serious critical questions to raise about his theoretical interpretation of the whole. The remaining sections of this chapter shall be devoted to those systematic issues in which Hartshorne's special perspective determines his contributions to process theology.

II

The problem of the continuity of individual life is the first issue. Let us assume the process commitment to events and agree with the claim that an enduring individual is an event-sequence. Chapter Two discussed continuity *within* events as genetic successiveness; the focus here is on continuity through and between events, coordinate transition, in Whitehead's words. The question is, what distinguishes those event-sequences that are *enduring individuals* from those that are not?

Whitehead's answer was that the event-sequence of an enduring individual has all its members characterized by a certain pattern, or by closely resembling patterns, whereas other event sequences do not. For instance, the event-sequence of a human being repeatedly exhibits the human arrangement of bodily parts, no matter how the person is postured in diverse events.

But the important kind of human continuity seems not to be organic, but rather mental. Prosthetic devices can replace parts of people's bodies, but they would still be themselves if their emotional and intellectual continuity was preserved. Yet conscious mental life is characterized by *novelty* of thought pattern, *not repetition.* Whitehead, in fact, made the point that repetition in the bodily environment for thought is the necessary prerequisite for creative novelty of imagination. Therefore, repetition of patterns cannot by itself account for continuity.

As Hartshorne points out, the event-sequences leading to mentally dominant events are generally of two basic types: memory and perception. A memorial event-sequence goes back through brain events, all of which belong to the remembering person. But perceptive event-sequences, by definition, are quickly traced out through the sense organs into the events of the environment explicitly not parts of the person. So, whereas the memorial event sequence repeats the remembered pattern through occasions all of which are parts of the person, a perceptive event sequence repeats the perceived patterns through a series some of whose members *in principle* are outside the person.

Then perhaps one's dominantly mental events are one's own, not so much because they repeat a pattern intrinsically, but rather becaue they feel themselves always to be taking place in the environment of one's body, and that body is perceived to have a repeating pattern. There is a profound phenomenological truth in this. One's feeling of continuity with one's past thoughts reflects a feeling for their common setting; as William James said, one's own thoughts seem "warm."

The feeling that all one's thoughts are *possessed by oneself* is not the only kind of continuity, however. Our experience seems committed to moral continuity. That is, one is obligated to keep promises made in the past, even if one has forgotten them. One is obligated in the present to plan the future so as to be able to be responsible for one's actions. And in less deontological kinds of situations, one conceives oneself as having a unique life, a career, with problems of life style and leading a meaningful life. These conceptions do not make much sense unless one's integral continuity is more than the embodiment of all one's thoughts in the same body.

These, of course, are common-sense suppositions about what the continuity of human life consists in. To take account of them I would suggest the event model of life be modified in the follow-

ing way. Let us distinguish among the data prehended in an event
in an enduring individual between essential and conditional data.
Essential data are factors determining the subjective form of the
event; conditional data are factors integrated by subjective form
but not significant for determining the subjective form itself;
there may be borderline data. Whitehead acknowledged what I
call essential data in only one case, that of the basic lure for subjective aim derived by a hybrid physical prehension of God. But
in an enduring individual such as a human being at least two and
perhaps three kinds of essential features are needed. First, there
must be essential features deriving from past events in one's life
that carry obligation from the past. Second, there must be essential features deriving from the future and binding one's present
actions in terms of norms for future consequences; these future-
derived essential features might be consciously anticipated, but
even if they are not one still is responsible for unanticipated consequences. Third, if the event in question involves free choice,
there may be essential features spontaneously arising as one com-
mits oneself to a value chosen; these are not of special concern
here. Now an enduring individual with personal integrity (as
either an ideal or an accomplishment) is an event-sequence any of
whose member events has essential data deriving from antecedent
and consequence members of the sequence. This difference between plain event-sequences and ones with enduring integrity is
a complication of the event model, but one that seems to be de-
manded by our common experience.

It is just at that last point, however, that Hartshorne would object. Perhaps our common experience is too narrow, biased in fact
by the implications of a surreptitious substance ontology. Perhaps we should be open to the Hindu experience that continuity,
when pressed, turns out to be the union of all in the world soul,
Atman. Perhaps with some Buddhists we should say continuity is
a mere appearance covering a mere multiplicity of flashes of reality. One of the greatest virtues Hartshorne sees in event-plural-
ism is that it does away with the metaphysical underpinning of
ego-centrism and the self-interest theory of motivation.[11] One
should make amends for one's own past wrongs; but it also makes
sense to say one should amend the past wrongs of the whole society. (Hartshorne says there is cogency in the claim that white

society should make restitution to blacks for past mistreatment by white society.) Likewise, one should aim for the future good of all events affected by one's present actions, not only those of one's own person. Refutation of ego-centrism and self-interest by denying the self, however, seems extreme surgery.

The critical point is not that Hartshorne has failed to account for continuity; his answer to that would be to deny the kind of continuity I have in mind. The critical point is that he has no argument I can find for his position on continuity. He cannot say that his position is strictly entailed by the event philosophy, because it is possible to sketch how an event philosophy can be amended to account for very strong kinds of continuity. He must say, then, that his theory better accounts for experience. But whose experience? He in fact suggests a reformation in our basic experience of individuality. To make out his position Hartshorne would have to deal extensively with the problem of which experiences are normative for theories and how theories give better or worse renderings of those experiences. For reasons having to do with his theory of apriori metaphysics, discussed below, he does not take up this question. We should conclude, therefore, that at least for some of us Hartshorne's event pluralism does not articulate our sense of individual continuity.

III

The second serious question concerns the claim made throughout *Creative Synthesis and Philosophic Method* that something abstract can be contained in something concrete. Hartshorne conceives the abstract and the concrete to be two poles, and the doctrine that the latter contains the former in his concept of dipolarity. Any event is dipolar, and most importantly, God is dipolar, containing an abstract and necessary nature in a concrete and existential state at any given time.

The use of the word *abstract* is unfortunate here, since it may well be question begging. It connotes that something abstract has been taken out of something larger and more concrete. But the truth of the matter may well be that something abstract merely is *known* because *an instance* of it is discovered in something concrete.

What sense does it make to say a universal is contained in a concrete particular? It is clear that an instance of a universal can be so contained. Perhaps it is better to say that the concrete particular itself is an instance of the universal, and perhaps of several other universals also. Or perhaps the preferable language is to speak of the particular as instancing the universal. But, however we say this, in what sense is the universal contained in the particular when the latter is an instance of it?

To this kind of question, two kinds of answers have been given falling within the "realist" camp. They can be called, for historical reasons, Aristotelian realism and Platonic realism.

An Aristotelian realist—and Hartshorne is one—holds that the problem of universals has to do with accounting for how similarities and identities develop in the concrete flow of events. Along with Peirce and Weiss, Hartshorne holds that particulars are completely determinate and therefore can only be past events, and that universals are somewhat indeterminate and can therefore characterize only the future. When universals are abstracted from the concrete particulars, characters are derived from the past as potentialities for future realization. In this sense, all potentiality derives from concrete actuality, an Aristotelian thesis. This makes sense of Hartshorne's contention, in his chapter "Abstraction: The Question of Nominalism," that the novel forms emergent in a creative event are not determinate before the event, but become determinate by decision in the event; to deny this is to deny any real meaning to creativity. For the Aristotelian position, the real problem is to explain how forms get into the temporal process, and it makes sense to say that they emerge.

An emergent universal is nonsense to a Platonist, however. For a Platonist the only things that can change or come to be are those essentially related to the existential temporal process, e.g., things that make decisions: events, and the like. A universal is that *by which we measure* change and diversity as well as continuity. As Plato argued in the *Parmenides*, instances of forms can be alike or similar, but there is no similarity between the instances and the universal itself; otherwise one gets into a third-man argument. So in a sense universals are not things, desiccated shapes imaging or being imaged in concrete particulars; rather they are norms, indeterminate in themselves, but determinate as measures of how the particular components of a complexity ought to go together. For a Platonist it is possible to abstract the pattern of a concrete thing and call it the form of the thing; but this is a shortcut to speaking the truth. The pattern is no more the universal than is the concrete thing so patterned; the only advantage of the pattern is that we can imagine it to be found in other particulars. But as Hartshorne, Weiss and others so well pointed out, concrete particulars always differ in their overall patterns; in fact, difference in concrete identity comes down to difference in determinate pattern. The universal or form itself is the value finding embodiment in the world in "a certain way." Two particulars are alike because the same value measures their similar components with a pattern ingredient in both. Their components are similar by virtue of being measured by the same component values, and so on down. The causal reason why things are similar may well be that they both prehend the same past events, and therefore have the same components to be measured in their own subjective forms. But the metaphysical reason for the possibility of similarity and difference, according to the Platonic realist, consists in the fact that value can be ingredient with multiplicity in different parts of a process only by virtue of different structures or patterns. As a Platonist would say, the structured world is a compromise between chaos and the Good. There is ultimately only one real universal, the Form of the Good; we distinguish different forms because there are similar patterns of complexities recurring and therefore exhibiting similar patterns, each of which seems to name a universal.[12]

Whereas the Aristotelian story is about how universals appear in the historical process—and in this sense they do seem to emerge—the Platonic story is about how determinateness is possible. Regarding the latter, a decision to make pattern X ingredient in oneself as a measure of components a, b, c . . . is not possible unless X is indeed a way of measuring a, b, c . . . together. Whether a, b, c . . . are measurable by X may be irrelevant to whether a, b, c . . . are actual in the temporal process. The relation between the pattern in which the form measures the pattern's components and the patterns of the components is eternal. Of course, if the components are never actualized in the real process, that relation is totally irrelevant to the course of events. But whether universals are relevant to the world makes no difference to the universals, conceived in this Platonic sense.[13]

The Aristotelian story of how the universals come to be relevant to and function in the worldly process of concrete events is not incompatible with the Platonic account of how change depends on its formal possibility. Platonists such as Whitehead provide theories about the ingression of forms in things through prehension of the past as well as theories about the constitution of formal possibility as such in terms of eternal objects, the divine primordial decision and the like. Whitehead unfortunately failed to emphasize the fact that eternal objects are norms, and had to say that eternal objects are empty except insofar as they are graded by God as relevant to the world. But his theory of propositional valuation is congenial for interpreting the eternal objects as norms, given determinate shape by the components they must measure together.

Aristotelians, however, have been less charitable in allowing the importance of both kinds of problems about universals. They assume that universals themselves must be like the instances of them in particulars, and then say the Platonic account ascribing independent existence to them is forced to believe in ghostly, wraithlike, disembodied essences. In discussing Platonism Hartshorne himself says, "I do not believe that a determinate colour is something haunting reality from all eternity, as it were, begging for instantiation. . . ."[14] In light of what the Aristotelians are trying to explain, universals can be treated as patterns derived from past actualities. But the function of universals to explain the Platonist's problem of formal possibility precludes their being conceived as proceeding from actuality; they are necessarily the antecedent condition of actuality. The Platonic universal for some determinate color is that value which would be actualized if some refracted light waves and some conditions of perception are patterned a certain way; in no sense does the universal beg for instantiation, although the concrete world might be better if the color were instantiated.

And so, whereas I have no important demurrers about the positive things Hartshorne says about universals, since he is giving a good account of the Aristotelian problem, his negative points are ill-taken. It is a great mistake to reject all Platonic theories of universals, such as Whitehead's regarding eternal objects (not that Whitehead's particular account is necessarily satisfactory). This mistake has serious ramifications for Hartshorne's view.

Consider his claim that the abstract is contained in the concrete exhaustively; that is, the union of the abstract and the concrete is simply the concrete. With respect to how universals are ingredient in the world, this presents no problem. Universals are structures in the past abstracted as potentialities for actualization in the present, and they have no reality in the world except as potentialities; the concrete realization of them contains them. But with respect to the formal possibility of those universal structures, Hartshorne's theory gives no account. That they are actually possible is not the issue, since they were actualized in the past. From the Platonist's side, the interesting question is why certain forms of togetherness are coherent and others not, why certain forms have great harmony and others little or none. Unless this kind of question is addressed, the ontological structure of the world is taken for granted, not made intelligible. Although the question of how this or that form gets ingredient in the world is interesting, the more interesting question is what structure is, how it unifies multiplicity, how it stands related to chaos.

Pushed far enough—and Hartshorne would surely push it that far—the claim that structure itself needs an explanation might be thought self-contradictory. First principles are structures, and what could lie behind a first principle? But then, as Peirce said, the only thing that does not need an explanation is pure chaos; order is most of all in need of explanation, and the explanation of a state of affairs in terms of first principles is not as penetrating as the explanation of the first principles themselves, as the previous chapter argued. Whereas Hartshorne cites Peirce's categories as illustrations of eternal metaphysical principles (in contrast to emerging ones), Peirce himself thought his categories of Firstness, Secondness and Thirdness *evolved*, evolution being the only way to explain the origin of order from chaos.[15] Whitehead in his turn, as Lewis S. Ford has pointed out, claimed that anything complex needs an explanation in a decision somewhere, and even the metaphysical structures of the world are the result of the divine primordial act giving order to the otherwise chaotic eternal objects.[16] Admitting that difficulties can be raised with both

Peirce's and Whitehead's accounts, some account of the formal possibility of potentialities is necessary beyond what Hartshorne can provide.

David A. Pailin has come to Hartshorne's defense against an early version of these criticisms. With respect to the present point, that Hartshorne needs to account for first principles themselves, Pailin makes two objections. What he calls his "practical" objection is that I seem "to be asking for a kind of ultimate metaphysical explanation which may well be beyond the competence of human understanding," and he cites God's response to Job out of the Whirlwind (Job 38:1-5a).[17] This objection holds only if an "ultimate metaphysical explanation" must be some yet higher determinate reason for what is to be explained. But, as pointed out at the end of the previous chapter, an alternate sense for "ultimate metaphysical explanation" is locating the decisive action that determines what is to be explained. Adopting this alternative sense, I can cite God's remarks to Job as indicative precisely of an instance of explaining first principles by reference to transcendent divine creative decision. Thus Pailin's objection presupposes a special view (one which I reject) about what an ultimate metaphysical explanation would have to be.

Pailin's second objection, one "in principle," is that it simply makes no sense to ask "for explanations of the basic principles of explanation. The nature of explanation, however, must presuppose such principles; otherwise explanation can never begin. Furthermore, in spite of Peirce it is not chaos but the principle of rationality that does not need explanation."[18] Pailin is surely correct that one cannot explain the principles of explanation starting from premises that do not presuppose that the principles are true. But my proposal is not that the explanation is a set of premises from which the explanandum is deduced. Rather, the explanation is a dialectical argument pointing to an act of creation that determines the explanandum.

One crucial part of that dialectical argument is the following consideration: What calls for explanation in an ordinary thing is its determinately complex character. We want to know how or why just these components are together in just the way they are. Whatever is determinately complex calls for explanation, because it can always be asked why that particular complexity has the determinate harmony or togetherness it has. Now "first principles" must be determinately complex. If they were not determinate, they would not show why there is any determinate character to what they explain. If they were not complex, they could not refer determinately and discriminatively to the complex components of those things they are supposed to explain. If "first principles" are determinately complex and if everything determinately complex calls for explanation, then "first principles" call for explanation. Peirce was right: Order (determinate complexity) does indeed call for explanation.

That the principles are "first" only locates their rank in an order of explanatory principles; it by no means entails that they do not call for explanation. To be sure, whatever would explain them could not be a yet more primordial determinately complex principle, for that would contradict the premise that they are "first." Perhaps it is the case, as Pailin (and Kant) urge, that "first principles" call for explanation but no explanation can be given. But that is contrary to fact, because explanation can be given by reference to a divine creative act which, apart from actually creating, would not be determinate or complex. It might be argued against explanation by reference to the creative act that such is not an explanation at all. But merely to point out that reference to the creative act is not an explanation by "first principles" is not to make that case; it is simply a different kind of explanation. Indeed, a kind of explanation different from that by "first principles" must be given to account for determinately complex "first principles."

Pailin's subtle defense to the contrary, I do believe that Hartshorne's theory suffers from its lack of an account for form itself.

IV

Consider the problem for Hartshorne's theory of God as dipolar in light of his lack of such an account. As Hartshorne has consistently maintained throughout his writings, the abstract nature of God consists in the apriori metaphysical conditions that would have to be exhibited in any possible world. He has argued in his many discussions of the ontological argument that the metaphysical possibilities for God are not only possible but necessary.[19]

That is, there must be some existing actual entity exhibiting the metaphysical conditions, although how that necessary existence is actualized relative to the contingencies of the other events in the world is itself a contingent matter. But now each occasion in the divine life is an instance of necessary existence. In what does the normative force of the necessity reside?

Any subsequent divine event would prehend the necessity in the antecedent divine event and have to exhibit it. But, I argue, if the necessity is completely contained as an abstract part of the antecedent divine event, there is no necessary reason for there to be *any* subsequent divine event to prehend it. Only if the abstract part of the divine nature is normative over *possible* divine events could those possible events be necessitated *before* they objectify the necessity prehended from their antecedents. But if such a situation obtained, then that transcendent normativeness could not be "contained" in any concrete divine event, only illustrated.

Of course it could be argued that, if the metaphysical conditions are necessarily existent, then *any* subsequent state of the world would have to illustrate them and would therefore be divine. But if the abstract necessity is completely contained in an antecedent divine state, with no transcendent normativeness, then there is no metaphysical reason to expect *any* subsequent events. Now Whitehead, though not Hartshorne, could argue that the Category of the Ultimate, involving creativity, would guarantee a new one out of any old many. But the dialectic in that Category of the Ultimate, involving creativity, many and one, would make it impossible to say in any sense that the Category is "contained" in a concrete actual entity, only illustrated there. Hartshorne cannot avail himself of the Category of the Ultimate as Whitehead did. In the long run even Whitehead's move does not help, as argued in the previous chapter. But it takes a step beyond Hartshorne.

Suppose Hartshorne were to grant that the metaphysical nature of God must be transcendent enough of any given concrete actualization of God to necessitate a successor divine occasion. He would ask whether this transcendence necessitates another kind of superdivine ontological being. Would we have to say, he would ask, that there is some eternal divine individual beyond the temporal divine career, necessitating the divine occasions "totum simul"? The answer to that question would be yes if and only if all universals, including normative ones, are real only in actual entities, as abstractions from their whole concreteness. That is, the answer is yes only if the Aristotelian account of universals alone is true. But the answer is no if we acknowledge a contrast between the sphere of actual things and the domain of norms as such. Norms are not individuals and they are not actualities; they are only instanced in actualities. If norms are something like eternal objects, not like actual entities, then their normativeness can bind the progress of the actual world without being transcendent individuals. Platonic realism does not entail that the form of the Good is an individual being. Only a view of universals like Hartshorne's would have to bear a transcendent individual as the actual locus of a transcendent metaphysical norm.

Pailin agrees that there is something confusing about Hartshorne's treatment of the abstract/concrete distinction in the case of God by means of the universal/instance distinction. He argues that, with respect to God (and perhaps elsewhere),

> the seat of the trouble is Hartshorne's use of the word "contain" since it tends to lead to a reflection of the two poles as if the abstract existence and concrete actuality of an event refer to two separate components which together comprise that particular event (cf. the container and what it contains) whereas they properly indicate a formal distinction needed for our understanding of both the self-identity of that event and its identity with other events to compose a temporally persistent object.[20]

Then, according to Pailin, it is possible to use the distinction between the reality of God and the formally distinct self-identity and relative identity to surmount the difficulties sketched above. The necessity of God, for instance, should not be conceived as located in the abstract nature (self-identity) but in God as such whom we know to be necessary. The continuity of God is not a problem in Pailin's view because, first, if there is a God the divine nature *must* be continuous and, second, since there is nothing beyond God to explain the divine continuity, the continuity must somehow consist in the divine reality as such. Because we know that God is "first" in explanation, God must be self-explanatory; that we cannot figure out how, except with "formal distinctions" that are paradoxical, poses no difficulty with God. It is only that we are asking to explain what we cannot explain:

> It may be a nice question whether and how God can know that his reality is intrinsically necessary and so unending, but nice questions of this order unfortunately seem to require speculations that are highly unlikely to be within our competence.[21]

What is the use of any speculative theology, however, if when it runs into conceptual difficulties it is declared to consist only of formal distinctions that are not expected to be explained anyway? *Any* theory of God whatsoever can say that its conceptual structures and arguments are only finite perspectives on God and then proceed to assert whatever dogmas are dearly beloved to be true of God's reality. At this point, the reference to God's reality is a *deus ex machina* alleged to ground assertions when rationality peters out. Hartshorne himself would never admit that his categories are mere formal distinctions or invoke the "divine reality" to save their collapse. In fact, Hartshorne maintains that our knowledge of God is literal, whereas most knowledge of creatures is qualified by imperfections.[22]

Nevertheless, if my arguments above are correct, then Hartshorne's notion of God as dipolar is much less useful than he thinks.

At best, God is dipolar in that the divine concrete nature contains instances of the normative principles that make God God, moment by moment. But the ontological status of those normative principles can by no means be reduced to the set of instances contained in the actual concrete events of the divine life.

V

If this conclusion is valid, then the far more important corollary is that the divine life Hartshorne calls God is not all it is made out to be. Beyond the divine life would be the normative metaphysical principles making it necessary that God instance them. And whatever transcendent status those metaphysical principles have as norms is a more interesting prospect for divinity than Hartshorne's candidate who, after all, is only infinitely inclusive and old, bound by necessity in essential nature, obliged to pay attention to all the rest of us without the possibility of shutting us off, and limited in creativity to choosing between only those alternatives having equal maximal value. (In this respect, Whitehead's God is no better off, unless Ford can make out his case, as discussed in Chapter Two, for a great status for God's primordial nature antecedent to the creation of the metaphysical categories or categoreal scheme.

Excepting problems with Whitehead's God, however, I want to make out a case for the advantages of his dualism of eternal objects and actual entities over Hartshorne's monism of concrete actual entities containing the universal forms as abstract parts. The case is developed not in terms of the internal dialectic of the logic of the systems, but rather in terms of their overall applicability to experience.

Whitehead argued rightly, and Hartshorne agrees, especially in the last chapter of *Creative Synthesis and Philosophic Method*, that value consists in intensity of experience and that intensity is a function of contrast. Generally put, contrast occurs when two things not fitting together according to their own internal principles are fitted together by the special context of the experiencer, by the subjective form that experiences them together. The contrast is greater the more the contrasted things are different and the less their real differences are compromised by the subjective form of their togetherness.

Human experience would have the greater contrast, prima facie, if some kind of dualism is true rather than some kind of monism. There is a metaphysically irreducible contrast in human experience if it is always a compromise between pure order and chaos, between normativeness and the unmeasured, between unifying structure and the plurality of things to be unified. For the sake of intensity of contrast in experience, it would seem to be more desirable that a Platonic metaphysics be true in which there is an irreducible dualism between Form and chaos, in which the realm of becoming is a measured compromise but still roiling with the forces of chaos, in which intelligibility belongs to the formal pole alone, chaos not needing an explanation, and the realm of becoming taking explanation only hypothetically.

But does experience indeed have this contrast? If so its marks would be in an irreducibility of contrast between the lasting and the perishing, between joy and anguish, between accomplishment and loss, between progress and tragedy. In other words, the peculiar coherence of fundamental ambiguity is a more intense contrast than the coherence of simply actualized positive fact. I place great metaphysical importance on suffering as well as satisfaction. The function of the Wailing Wall in old Jerusalem is one of the profoundest insights of religion, and it has its counterparts in other cults. To put the point in Western theological language, glorifying God is an activity essentially sustaining a basic contrast between lamentation and thanksgiving.

Is this basically religious vision of things aimed at the truth? Hartshorne would probably say no. According to his conception, nothing really perishes from God's memory; the world is fundamentally cumulative and lasting. Although anguish may be the momentary state, by metaphysical necessity God must objectify it in divine infinite felicity. Tragedy can only be a short-run view. To say the short run is all a human being may have, and that the tragedy *for the person* is irreducible, still lacks poignancy. As Hartshorne says, and I agree, altruism is human beings' natural estate because they identify with the good of all their successor events, not only those that can be named with their own name. If this is so, Hartshorne's denial of perishing means future divine felicity amends any present suffering, no matter how far in the future. My own religious intuitions tell me that, if God wipes away the tears, it is out of divine freedom, not because God is metaphysically obliged. The depth of my experience, and that of people through the ages and across all cultures, is slighted by metaphysical resolutions of its ambiguity. If the ambiguity is not the last word, at least its resolution should be by creative free choice, and our metaphysics should reflect this possibility.

VI

It is always disappointing when a philosopher has to appeal to ultimate intuitions. Let me return to more dialectical ground. In one of the most interesting chapters of *Creative Synthesis and Philosophic Method*, "The Prejudice in Favour of Symmetry," Hartshorne argues that the metaphysical debate between monists and pluralists regarding internal and external relations has resulted from construing the primary forms of relations to be symmetrical. He undertakes an ingenious logical argument showing that asymmetry is more basic than symmetry, and that equality can be defined in terms of inequality. The asymmetry Hartshorne has in mind as cosmologically significant is in his interpretation of causal process. An event constitutes, and is then perceived by, a later event. It is a condition for the later event, although the later event does not figure in its own constitution except in unusual cases of conscious anticipation. So we can say that, in the causal relation, the effect is external to the cause and the cause internal to the effect. In perception, the object perceived is internally related to the perceiver; but the perceiver is externally related to the perceived.

As we have come to expect, the dual transcendence consists in the fact God is universally necessary in abstract character and universally relative in concrete contingent character, these two sides being "reconciled by the old principle that the concrete contains the abstract."[23] The point is that any finite event, with its evil and suffering, is externally related to the future events rectifying it. But the future events contain the past events as rectified, as best as possible. So Hartshorne concludes there is no "problem of evil." This does not mean there is no evil in the world. Rather, the evil is the result of finite choices other than God's. But God takes up the evil and makes the best of it in subsequent divine events. So, although there is a lasting fact of evil, no evil itself lasts as evil. All evil puts unchangeable conditions on the future; but the future can make the best of those conditions and it has infinite resources for that task. Again, my intuitions are that this makes things too easy.

The moral I would draw is that Hartshorne should not have taken symmetry as his argument point (although I do not object to his arguments there). Rather he should have taken up the claims of metaphysical dualism mentioned above. While the course of the world might go on with the asymmetrical causation Hartshorne describes, it also goes on, I believe, as a compromise between norms and chaos. So the present does not unambiguously include the past; it loses a little, perhaps sometimes the most important parts. And the present cannot content itself with a freedom external to the future, knowing that the future will inevitably consume it.

The reason I believe in the dualist theory is that it seems to do better prima facie justice to experience, and Hartshorne should consider it. At the very least, we would be more in his debt if he could show experientially that the ambiguities of life are *not* to be taken at face value, and that experience is properly to be interpreted as his system calls for.

VII

This brings me to a final main issue. Hartshorne is a great believer in apriori knowledge. Apriori truths are those that must be illustrated by any possible world. There are two kinds of positive claims for him: those to which there are positive alternatives and those for which positive alternatives are inconceivable. The former are empirical claims, the latter apriori metaphysical ones. Yet the latter are not mere tautologies of the sort that, once one denies the subject one can deny the predicate. On the contrary, it is contradictory to deny the subject. Of course, the positive apriori metaphysical affirmation might be completely meaningless; one needs a metaphysical system to show that the apriori claim is at least conceivable. But with such an interpretive scheme, if an apriori truth is conceivable, it is inconceivable that the world exist without it. Furthermore, as positive the claim is verified in *every* experience.

At the heart of these claims by Hartshorne is his defense of the ontological argument. Along with Pailin I have no quarrel with the validity of the ontological argument; but we share grave doubts about what the argument proves. Assuming that the ontological argument does prove that we contradict ourselves if we say God is not necessary, does that in itself prove that there is a God? Pailin argues that it does not because it would require the further and unprovable premise that reality corresponds to our rational necessities.

> To affirm on this basis that God does exist involves the further and controversial step of maintaining that there is sufficient correspondence between what is the case in itself and our understanding of it

so that what satisfies our metaphysical understanding of reality reflects its actual structure. . . . Metaphysical thought, that is, can only seek satisfying understanding by assuming the reality of that in which it will find such finality.[24]

Pailin's objection is not entirely persuasive to me because I cannot quite formulate his distinction between "what is the case" and "our understanding of it" without presupposing some standards of rationality, a presupposition which begs the question in the distinction. Probably the reason I cannot formulate the distinction is that Pailin shares with Hartshorne but not with me a view of the apriori character of rationality that gives it a life of its own independent of experiential interactions with "what is the case." More of this shortly.

Pailin does argue that Hartshorne's treatment of the ontological argument possesses two signal virtues, even if it does not establish the reality of God, and my difficulties with the argument are difficulties with these virtues. Hartshorne's first insight, according to Pailin, is in his claim that the ontological argument shows that our real choice is between believing that "there is a God and that 'reality' makes sense in some metaphysical manner, whether or not we can ever grasp what that sense is, and holding that there is no God and that any apparent metaphysical understanding of reality can only be an illusion which does not significantly correspond to the ultimate nature of things."[25] Further, Hartshorne has shown that this is a genuine choice by refuting those objections to the theistic position that claim the concept of God is incoherent. My difficulty is that I do not see that Hartshorne has developed a coherent conception of God, for reasons cited throughout this discussion. In terms of the ontological argument, Hartshorne has *not* shown that God is possible, and thus should not conclude that God is necessary (which would of course follow if God is not contingent and also not impossible). It would seem to be still debatable whether the rationality of reality requires that there be a theistic structure.

The second virtue Pailin claims for Hartshorne's treatment of the ontological argument is that the logical status of claims about God is shown to be apriori. That is, God is shown to be compatible with all possible worlds, and claims about God are not falsifiable. From this Hartshorne concludes that the alternatives to theism are positivism or apriori atheism. But is this an advance, from the standpoint of defending theism? Would it not be better to relate as much as possible of God's character to the world so that experience generally will tend to corroborate and reinforce theological claims? Hartshorne would answer in the negative because of his strong view of apriori truths. There are, however, two lines of difficulty with that conception of apriori truth that I cannot escape.

First, Hartshorne treats the matter almost exclusively from the standpoint of *logica docens*. That is, he discusses apriori truths from the standpoint of their having been discovered, with the only problem being to clarify them. One might assume that this clarification is the discovery of them in the first place. But it makes good logical sense to say that, as elements of human knowledge, the so-called apriori truths are mere hypotheses about the universal conditions of existence. Hartshorne need not deny this. But then what we have in mind in thinking the truths are simply hypotheses, with varying degrees of plausibility. They are hypotheses *about* universal conditions. But the conditions are not apriori; apriori refers to a modality of truth claims, whether they are known to be true apart from experience, or from experience. Are the truths themselves apriori if they are hypotheses?

It may be impossible to conceive of an alternative to the claim that "whatever is a universal condition for any possible world is an apriori truth." But it surely is possible to conceive of alternatives to any candidate for such a truth. Therefore it can only be a hypothesis that such and such a claim (for instance that the necessity proved by the ontological argument is a concrete actual being) is a universal condition. Now how is that kind of hypothesis to be probated? By logic? Of course not, if it is conceivable that there are alternatives. (I hope to have shown above that there are very serious alternatives to Hartshorne's conception of dipolar deity even within such neighboring philosophies as Whitehead's.) Then is the hypothesis probated by experience? Not by any critical or finite experience, perhaps; in this, philosophy differs from the exact science. *But neither by being exemplified in all experiences,* because the very hypothesis at issue is whether all experiences are to be *interpreted* according to this hypothesis rather than some other. After all, the only alternative to a given hypothesis about a universal condition of experience would have to be a hypothesis that equally well claimed to interpret *all* experiences. So the decision would be made between the given hypothesis and some other(s) regarding which made the *best* interpretation of *all* experiences. An alternative failing to interpret some finite set of experiences would not be a real alternative.

But the *truth ascertained by the process of probating the hypotheses* certainly would not be apriori, even if the truths are about universal and necessary conditions. And what criteria do we employ in determining the "best interpretation of experience"? To some extent we can use formal criteria of elegance, simplicity and fruitfulness. I wish Hartshorne had concentrated more attention on this problem.

For the most part, however, we employ appeals to our inarticulate, pervasive, and life-orienting experience. And the "our" here means sometimes oneself, sometimes the whole race. Our experience of course is not completely inarticulate, being made sophisticated by having been carved up by dozens of subtle philosophical tools. But there is always a difference between experience rendered by a philosophy and experience judging the rendering. The latter cannot be stated by itself—and therefore is inarticulate. But it is recalcitrant, though corrigible, and thereby keeps us honest and wise, if not smart. I wish that Hartshorne had paid more attention to the sense in which experience is the final arbiter. Sometimes it seems he does not believe it. This is my second difficulty.

The Hartshornean candidates for apriori truths rest, it seems to me, on an experiential sense too much refined by his philosophy. In other words, I suspect his experience confirms his theory, but his experience may be too narrow. This criticism is really at best a hypothesis: Do the readers feel as I do that ambiguity, suffering and perishing have a more substantial place in human experience than rendered by Hartshorne's philosophy? (Hartshorne's discussion of the role of experience in philosophical method treats only memory and perception, not at all what life "adds up to."[26])

Of course, Hartshorne would answer that, if the truth is metaphysical, it is embodied in any possible experience and therefore has no empirical force. He might even claim that, if a metaphysical truth made a difference to the way one experiences the world, it is an empirical claim in disguise. But surely it must make a difference to understand what the apriori conditions of existence are! At least the understanding should make us wiser. But if the metaphysical truths suggested have the effect of flattening our experience, of solving our problems with metaphysical necessities, of relieving our cares with confidence in principle instead of with felt concrete redemption, then his metaphysics impoverishes experience. And I know of no way of defining truth so independent of value that a metaphysical scheme could be said to be true if it leaves your experience less rich than it found it.

Pailin strenuously objects to this point, arguing that instead of appeals to "richness" versus "impoverishment" "one structure of understanding is to be preferred to another ... primarily on the grounds that it provides a more correct awareness and account."[27] But this supposes a correspondence view of the relation between understanding and its object that is belied by the nature of philosophical argument. In practice we deal with many hypotheses, all of which can "admit" the same realities but which differ by attributing different kinds of importance and connections to things. How do we choose between such hypotheses except on pragmatic grounds? Does not our long-range judgment on a philosophy take the form of judging whether or not it captures the living waters of experience?

VIII

A subtle undercurrent within the tradition of process theology is brought to the surface by an objection Pailin makes to the contrast sketched between Hartshorne's conception of God and the conception of God as creator *ex nihilo*. To claim, as I have, that God transcends the categories illustrated in temporal process because those very categories are divinely created, is to deny several connotations traditionally associated with theism. This rouses the hackles of Pailin's apologetic theology.

What Neville does not seem to recognize sufficiently is that theistic faith demands an understanding of God who is the object of its faith and worship . . . and, furthermore, that it generally demands a coherent concept of God who is not only the ontologically, valuatively, and rationally other but also an individual reality who instantiates these qualities in a personal mode of being. For Neville, therefore, to dismiss apparently out-of-hand the view that God is significantly to be described as individual, actual, and knowledgeable is for him to show that when he is talking about "God" he is not talking about the object of theistic faith and worship.[28]

To this, several responses need to be made. The genuine theological issue is which conception of God is best, not which one corresponds to the "object of theistic faith and worship" which, for all that, might be false. Furthermore, insofar as philosophical theology needs to do justice to experience, it needs to do justice to all experience, not the selective experience of theists. If there are as many difficulties with the process conception of God as "individual, actual, and knowledgeable" as I have argued, then it is not out-of-hand to prefer another conception.

Moreover, by what right do the defenders of the conception of God as an individual (etc.) lay exclusive claim to the privileges of the rhetoric of theism? Surely mystical and apophatic traditions have denied that conception and still thought of themselves as theists. Divinity school theologians such as Tillich have been theists while claiming that God is not an individual. But by what right does anyone lay claim to a label for oneself? If future scholars decide that the historical label of theism should not be applied to those who deny that God is a determinate individual, then so be it. What counts is a view's cogency and faithfulness to life, not its name or associations. I doubt that Hartshorne would share Pailin's concern to develop a conception for the sake of defending the faith of theism.

These disclaimers notwithstanding, process theology has achieved much of its present status by its claim to offer a better logical grounding for the God of Western religions than the older conceptions. The issue of historical associations cannot be dismissed. Two American theologians of great distinction have developed process theology for its advantages over other conceptions for religious purposes. Shubert Ogden has argued its superiority over what he calls the "classical" conception in the West. John B. Cobb, Jr., has used process theology to offer a conceptual framework with a perspective on the major world religions. Chapters Five and Seven will take up these views.

·V·

God as Neoclassical

Shubert M. Ogden, along with John B. Cobb, Jr., pioneered the deployment of process theism as a conceptual vehicle for Christian theology, working explicitly within a seminary context. His *Reality of God* made process theology a decisive option within Protestant thinking at a time when Karl Barth's neo-orthodoxy seemed to be the only authentic mode of theological thinking.[1] His views have also been taken up with great vigor and general approval by David Tracy, the distinguished Roman Catholic theologian.[2]

The initial attraction of Ogden's position is that process categories allow us to make sense of the secular world while maintaining the heart of Christian convictions. The classical categories of Christian philosophy, those developed in the European medieval period, are incapable of recognizing the authentic truth in secular experience. The categories of process theism, which do allow that recognition, are thus to be called neoclassical. Furthermore, besides being philosophically respectable, neoclassical metaphysics accords well with the biblical description of God, according to Ogden, and thus opens the way for a properly secular Christianity.

I

What is Ogden's analysis of secular culture? He characterizes it as "emphatic affirmation that man and the world are themselves of ultimate significance."[3] Can we question whether this affirmation is well taken? Ogden says that "one thing, it would appear, in which almost all of us today share is just our experience as modern, secular men: our affirmation of life here and now in the world in all its aspects and in its proper autonomy and significance."[4] Now it is true that socialized beings participate willy-nilly in their culture; that is what makes them human and historical. But it is not accurate to assume that sharing in the culture means accepting it; a person also can try to reform it in parts, perhaps even at its base. Since it is the intellectual's task to determine what our responses to culture's many facets *ought* to be, it is an invalid argument to say simply that religion ought to conform to cultural requirements.[5] It depends on the requirements. Ogden says, for instance, that "commitment to secularity entails acceptance of logical self-consistency as one of the necessary conditions for the truth of any assertion"; self-consistency undoubtedly is a good thing and whatever in secularity promotes it should be supported.[6] But whether persons and the world ought to be accorded ultimate significance, even assuming that secularity says they have it, cannnot be decided merely by citing secularity's claims. Independent assessments of contemporary movements would, I believe, support most of what Ogden prizes without appealing to authority (a kind of appeal *not* prized in secularism).

Ogden by no means thinks of the secular world as monolithic. He distinguishes the general secularity of the modern age from secular*ism*, the belief that the ultimate significance of the world excludes any legitimate reference to a transcendent divinity. He discusses this in the areas of knowledge and morals, arguing that Humeans and other secularists exclude *knowledge* of the transcendent, and that many Kantians (though not Kant) exclude reference to a transcendent ground for *morality*. Ogden claims that the limitations of secularism excluding reference to God are illegitimate, and argues on both epistemological and moral fronts.[7]

The reason secularists reject the possibility that the concept of God is meaningful, he says, is that they reject a particular metaphysics of God that in fact ought to be rejected, namely, the classical one.[8] They do this on Humean grounds, claiming that there can be no empirical evidence for a transcendent God. But they mistakenly believe, says Ogden, that the difficulties in the classical view do away with all metaphysics, rendering any concept of a transcendent God meaningless. Ogden's attack, then, is directed at the Humean empirical verifiability principle.

I fear this is a strategic blunder on Ogden's part. It is always of utmost importance to locate one's true opponents, and in terms of epistemology Hume is not the villain with respect to the knowledge of God. Kant is. According to Kant, objects can be known only through empirical means or through the conditions for the possibility of their being objects for knowledge in the first place. Now Ogden admits that God cannot be known empirically. But if Kant is right, then any kind of God that might be part of the conditions for the possibility of knowledge and so known that way could not be transcendent. The Kantian tradition has quite properly drawn the conclusion that nothing so much a part of human subjectivity ought to be called God. This is a much harder opponent to combat. Ogden's tactic against the Humeans is to laud Charles Hartshorne's theory that metaphysical statements are analytic and positive at once; because their contradictories are self-contradictory, metaphysical statements are logically true and determinative of all possible worlds. No Kantian would accept this, however, since logical statements as such have no objects, and can be given objects only through the conditions of empirical intuition, conditions God could not meet. Until Ogden refutes the Kantian contention that logic is *merely* forms of relations of ideas, and not knowledge, he has not faced the source of the secularistic skepticism about God. We shall return to consider the Kantian problem in the following chapter.

Let us turn now to a central thesis of Ogden, namely, that people necessarily have faith in God, even if only an implicit faith. Ogden recognizes clearly the distinction between the reflective level of the mind and the existential level of the heart and notes that, although the two influence each other, the problems of faith are different for each. But he claims that in the heart there is no such thing as lack of faith in God, only true faith and various kinds of positive distortions.[9] This, however, is in contradiction to what he had said earlier about the secularistic person. A secularist is someone whose participation in modern culture leads to seeing no significance in anything transcending certain narrowly defined limits of experience. This kind of person, I submit, has no faith. The secularist does not divide ultimate loyalty between God and some idol; there is no ultimate loyalty, since ultimacy is not meaningful.[10]

Ogden might argue that the epistemological limitations of secularistic culture apply only to the reflective level; but this would be unpersuasive. It would contradict the contention that reflective atheism "tends to pervert the heart as well as the mind."[11] Furthermore, it would plainly be contrary to the experience we have of the "fool who says in his heart there is no God," even when he knows reflectively from Anselm that that is inconceivable. It would have been a great help if, in proving that faith is unavoidable, Ogden would deal with the kind of experiential atheism he cited as characteristic of secularism.

Ogden's argument is that, when people suppose anything to be meaningful, they suppose that there is a God. He argues this in detail regarding morality, adopting Stephen Toulmin's contention that there are limiting questions to morality that are really religious. The argument for calling them religious questions is that the function of faith is to provide reassurance and, in the case of morality, the limiting questions call for reassurance that doing the good is meaningful, that it is significant to keep promises, and the like.[12] Ogden argues that religion reassures by re-presenting an original ground of confidence that people had not been aware of. He then argues, departing from Toulmin, that this implies the condition of any significant activity such as moral action to be an original confidence. People would never be involved enough in the moral sphere to get to the limiting questions unless they already had a confidence in the meaningfulness of their activity.

This seems a somewhat shaky argument, however. People often take dimensions of life such as morality to have significance because convention, tradition and prudence teach them to; and when these get called into question many people lose confidence and despair of all meaning. Some of them may respond to religion; but this may be either because religion functions simply as a new convention, or because it presents an *original* confidence. For many people there is no confidence prior to religion that religion can re-present. If religion is to provide a ground for faith it must be able to present the ground originally, it seems to me, not as something already presupposed. This is the significance of the tradition of the Holy Spirit and the presence of the Kingdom of God in Christianity, and there are parallels in other traditions.

Ogden suggests that the fragmentary life lived by someone who sees no significance in it cannot be given a systematic reflective account.[13] This I think is true. It may also be true that the ontological argument is valid, which means that one cannot reflectively be an atheist. But none of this proves that people cannot be atheists in their hearts, or that they cannot live without faith. In fact those despairing souls who find little or no significance in life probably will not pursue the demands of intellectual completeness to their limits to discover the discrepancy between what the mind is forced to acknowledge and what the heart feels.

I have a brief general reservation about the *intention* to show that faith is unavoidable, quite apart from Ogden's failure, to my mind, to fulfill it. He very wisely opens the book with the comment that the question of the existence of God has returned to the center of intellectual inquiry and in fact to the center of culture. But if his subsequent analysis is correct, then the reality of God is a real problem only on the reflective level, since there can be no question of divine reality in the heart, only of how we are to believe in him.[14] Is this not a great blindness to the real issue? God is first a problem for the heart, and only secondarily for reflection. The failure to see this marks the failure to see the challenge of secularity in the modern age.[15]

II

Ogden writes,

> We have seen that the only God whose reality is implied by a secular affirmation is the God who is the ground of confidence in the ultimate worth or significance of our life in the world. Given this affirmation, God must be so conceived that his being this ground of confidence is rendered as intelligible as possible. This requires, in turn, that our conceptuality, or system of fundamental concepts, enable us to think of his nature as defined by two essential characteristics.[16]

Let us examine these characteristics. "First, God must be conceived as a reality which is genuinely related to our life in the

world and to which, therefore, both we ourselves and our various
actions all make a difference as to its actual being."[17] Ogden takes
it as the great failing of the classical tradition that it can make no
sense of the world's relation to God. He quotes Aquinas to the
effect that in God there is no real relation to creatures.[18] But even
supposing that this complaint is appropriate against Aquinas, it
does not follow that this condemns the whole classical tradition.
Any garden variety creation theory would say that God's character is constituted in part by what God creates; God is a "this sort
of world type creator" rather than a "that sort of world type
creator." The least difference in the world makes a difference in
God. I suspect Ogden means more by "real relation" than "making a difference," but it needs to be spelled out.

There is a kind of relation, that for technical purposes can be
called a "real" relation, wherein two things are related so that
each has some features stemming from and conditional upon the
other, and also some features essential to itself and independent of
the other. The distinction between conditional and essential features was explored earlier. Two things really related in this way
would be internally constituted in part by each other and still
maintain integrity over against each other. Another kind of relation, however, obtains between two things, one of which is the
creator of the whole being of the other. The created thing would
in fact be a feature of the creator, in the sense that it would have
no features of its own that are not the product of the creator's
creation. The created thing would have no integrity *over against*
the creator, since over against the creator it would have no being;
but it would have the integrity of being exactly what the creator
creates it to be. The creator would have features pertaining to
being creator, to the created product it holds in being, and to its
act of creating; all these are relative to what is created precisely
because the product is completely dependent on the creator, not
in spite of that. Now classical theology has construed God to be
related to the world in something like the creator-created way.
Ogden, however, thinks the other sort of relation somehow is entailed by secularity. To my mind, he fails to demonstrate this. At
any rate, the neoclassical conception of God involves real relations, but not of creator-created type.

The second requirement Ogden offers is that

... we can think of God only as a reality whose relatedness to our life is itself relative to nothing and to which, therefore, neither our own being and actions nor any others can ever make a difference as to its existence.[19]

Ogden explains that, no matter what God actually happens to be relative to, it is necessary that God exist as relative to whatever happens to be. Necessary existence is no bone of contention with classical theologians, nor is necessary relation if that is interpreted as, "given creation, God is necessarily related to what God creates." Classical theology in many of its forms, however, balks at certain relations being necessary—for instance, God's relation to the world as its redeemer, lover and so forth. Those relations are a matter of grace, not necessity, in much traditional theology. Ogden seriously qualifies the creation relation, unfortunately, and does believe that the relations of grace are relations of necessity; I shall return to this point in discussing the religious difficulties with his view.

At this stage in Ogden's argument there is a lacuna. Somehow he must show what the ground of confidence in the ultimate worth or significance of life has to do with God. Despite what he says, neither of his requirements, if met, would make the connecting link between the ground of confidence and God. Suppose God is necessarily related; that just means the world registers in God, not that it is worth much or is significant. Suppose God also is related necessarily; that just means God cannot turn us off, not that the world adds up to anything of worth or significance. The argument depends on an equivocation in the word *significant*. It can mean "determinative" (and in this sense the world is significant for God); but it can also mean "important" or "valuable," and the latter meaning is not analytically entailed by the former. To make a difference to God has nothing to do with the value of the world, at least directly, according to what Ogden has shown.

There seems to be another important logical mistake in Ogden's strategy. He does not see that the significance of life and the world must be a character *of that life and world*, some property internal to it, not a property of God's knowledge. Ogden simply supplies no reason to believe that God's relativity to the world bestows significance; for all the machinery of neoclassical metaphysics he wants to insist upon, it could still be intricately related vanity.

It is worthwhile here to recall process philosophy's conception of the relation between God and the world to see why Ogden might think that reference to God solves the problem of significance. The fundamental unit of reality is an occasion of actual experience, a process of bringing to actuality an arrangement of prehensions, or, in Ogden's rather good phrase, "immediate sympathetic feelings" of other antecedent actual occasions.[20] At the finish of the moment there is a pattern actualized and as such it is a datum for the prehension of later occasions. The reality in itself of each unit of experience, however, is not the actuality but the process of bringing the actuality to be; Whitehead called this reality in itself "subjective reality," the reality of the subject in the process of experiencing. As actualized, the pattern is only an object for other occasions' prehensions, what Whitehead called "objective reality"; objective reality, or actualized experience, has no reality in itself. Whereas the actual occasions of human experience only prehend a limited range of objects, God necessarily experiences every other occasion and does so perfectly, omitting or suppressing nothing. In this sense, everything that happens has an inexpungible place in God's experience.

The problem of value has to do with the kind of arrangement of prehensions in experience. According to Whitehead, those arrangements that are more densely packed with greater contrasts harmonized together are better. Human experience is such that human beings must exclude or suppress much that could be prehended just in order to get a harmonious arrangement; God, by contrast, is able to include everything and always get the best possible arrangement of experience. According to neoclassical metaphysics, God's concrete reality is the process whereby, through each moment of divine experience, God harmonizes whatever the world offers to be prehended in the best possible way. In this sense God is necessarily supreme, although perfectly relative to what the world offers in a given present. The items in the world at subsequent occasions prehend God and note what God has done with the divine antecedents, taking this as a lure for their own arrangement.

I suspect what Ogden has in mind by relating significance to the God of process philosophy is that he takes faith in significance to mean faith that our experience will not be forgotten by God and that God will enhance it by what is combined with it in the divine experience. This, however, is beside the point. Life is significant because of the pattern of the harmonies of prehensions; this is as true of finite experience as of divine, the difference being only that finite experience could be improved whereas the divine cannot be. Ogden's problem is *whether* there is significance, not whether it has a divine degree.

Furthermore, according to the Hartshornean tradition of process philosophy, an occasion cannot pass away subjectively into actuality without being objectively prehended; therefore, if there were no God, some other finite occasion would prehend it, and be prehended in turn indefinitely, always having significance in the sense of making a difference. True, people would be prehended in ways that do less than the best with them, and this may be a source of concern. God's perfect prehension is equally a source of concern, however, in that God by metaphysical necessity must be perfectly just; God cannot forget evil or forgive sins, only make the best of them.

III

Ogden claims that the classical conception of God is contradictory, and that the neoclassical conception is not. I want first to indicate that his fundamental arguments against the old view do not hold, and then to show that his own view has its share of contradictions. In neither case need my arguments be exhaustive, but instead just hit the central points.

Ogden argues first that the traditional conception contradicts itself in claiming on the one hand that

> God creates the world freely, as the contingent or nonnecessary world our experience discloses it to be. . . . At the same time, because of their fixed commitment to the assumptions of classical metaphysics, theologians also tell us that God's act of creation is one with his own eternal essence, which is in every respect necessary, exclusive of all contingency. Hence, if we take them at their own

word, giving full weight to both of their assertions, we at once find ourselves in the hopeless contradiction of a wholly necessary creation of a wholly contingent world.[21]

Ogden's conclusion is unfortunately invalid, an example of bad logic. It is not at all contradictory to say that the world is wholly contingent in the sense that it needs a cause other than itself in order to exist at all, and that God the cause necessarily produces its effect. This is only to say that without the cause the effect would not exist, but that with the cause it must exist.

Ogden might want to say the word *contingent* merely means "not necessary," and that therefore the created world is not contingent if there is a necessary cause of it. But there is a distinction to be drawn between the world considered by itself and the world considered with God its creator. The world *with* God is necessary, on the classical supposition, and the necessity derives from the divine cause. The world considered by itself, however, is contingent, needing a cause if it is to exist at all. Now in the first sentence of the quote Ogden indicates the contingency to apply to the world alone, not to the world plus God: Our experience is of the world. In this sense it is possible to have a "wholly necessary creation of a wholly contingent world," the contingency of the world consisting in the fact that, apart from actually being caused, it would not be. There would be no point in contrasting necessary creation with contingent world if the world were not to be considered in distinction from the creator.

The issue Ogden means to raise has to do with the cause alone, whether it produces its effect freely or necessarily; in either case the effect would be contingent, and the experience of contingency he cites is not relevant. The Christian motive for holding to free creation has chiefly been to account for the belief that creation is a matter of voluntary grace; this requires that sense be given to the claim that God could do otherwise than create, just as God could do otherwise than redeem. The *classical* question of the priority of will and nature in God deals with just this issue; if God's nature is prior and determined to create, then the will is necessary, and so is creation; if God's will is prior, then nature is derivative from willing and creating, and the divine creation is not necessary. Perhaps Thomists would be unhappy with this latter solution (and Ogden often identifies the classical conception of God with Thomism), but there are other classical conceptions that could admit that God's character is constituted by God's action, just as persons constitute themselves by what they do. This is well expressed by the creator-created relation discussed above.

Ogden's second main argument is that the traditional conception of God has maintained

> that the end of man is to serve or glorify God through obedience to his will and commandments. And yet the God whom we are thus summoned to serve is, in the last analysis, so conceived that he can be as little affected by our best actions as by our worst. As *actus purus*, and thus a statically complete perfection incapable in any respect of further self-realization, God can be neither increased nor diminished by what we do, and our action, like our suffering must be in the strictest sense wholly indifferent to him.[22]

This criticism supposes that *actus purus* is a substance distinct from the world, and perhaps there are theologians who have thought that way. Most theologians, however, have thought of God as the creator who is immediately present in the being of the creatures; the creatures are the *termini* of God's creative act, and as such their welfare is the welfare of the divine reality itself present through God's creative act in creatures. Although it is not possible in this view to say, as Ogden wants, that God waits to see what we do and then responds, it is also impossible to say God is indifferent since God's very character depends on divine creation. It is yet another question to ask how people can serve God if God cannot be improved. But Ogden refers to the answer himself; people serve God by glorifying God.[23] This does not improve God, it only gives the divine glory. God is not better off with more glory rather than less; it is just better to glorify God than not, since that is what human betterment is in classical Christian conceptions.

Let us now examine the concept of God Ogden would suggest.

> The starting point for a genuinely new theistic conception is what Whitehead speaks of as "the reformed subjectivist principle." According to this principle, we can give an adequate answer to the

metaphysical question of the meaning of "reality" only by imaginatively generalizing "elements disclosed in the analysis of the experience of subjects." In other words, the principle requires that we take
as the experiential basis of all our most fundamental concepts the
primal phenomenon of our own existence as experiencing subjects
or selves.[24]

It should be noted at the outset that Ogden's "in other words" says
something quite different from Whitehead's words. The latter's
point was that the elements of philosophical abstraction must derive from experience and therefore must be found in experiencing
subjects.[25] In contrast, Ogden wants to claim that we should take
human selves as the model for real entities. Ogden really under-
stands the situation as a Thomistic existentialist, accepting the
existentialist notion of a subject and then reasoning to other entities by conceiving them on the analogy with oneself. In this sense
his praise of process philosophy is misleading, because he only
uses process models for quite old-fashioned purposes. He believes
that philosophy works by paradigm, classical philosophy working
on the paradigm of objective entities like tables and chairs, neoclassical philosophy on the paradigm of "existing subjects"; that
he has the existentialist view in mind is shown by his insistence
on *existing* subjects—for an ordinary paradigm, a nonexisting
subject would do, not necessarily the inner view of oneself.[26] Of
course, if any real philosophy is in fact determined as much by
the paradigm argument as Ogden thinks, it would be simply
naive, running afoul of the simplest paradoxes of representative
perception and knowledge of other minds. Fortunately, neither
classical philosophy nor process philosophy does this.

The analogy Ogden has in mind for God is the relation of our
selves to our bodies. He claims that our selves "participate by immediate sympathetic feeling" in our bodies, most particularly in
our brain cells.[27] The human self has a very limited capacity for
such direct relatedness. God is a self that participates by immediate sympathetic feeling in every actual thing in the world, supreme in that God is perfectly related and yet sensibly
determined by everything there is. God is temporal and growing
in perception of temporal and growing things. Ogden also insists
that the divinity is creative, but not in the sense that God creates

the world; rather, an entity is creative by organizing what it prehends into new patterns that then become constituents of later entities.

Following Whitehead and Hartshorne, Ogden calls his conception of God "dipolar," one pole abstract and the other concrete. In abstract essence God is absolute and supreme; concretely God is related to all. Ogden hopes this to solve all the problems of the infinite and finite, the necessary and the contingent, the eternal and the temporal, the absolute and the relative.[28] That he makes almost no attempt to justify these hopes can be excused in large part because Charles Hartshorne has been most thorough, intelligent, and courageous in his attempt to justify them, and Ogden apparently does not differ significantly from Hartshorne whose views were examined in the previous chapter.

Certain internal difficulties ought to be pointed out in the neoclassical theory, focusing this time on Ogden's rather than Hartshorne's expression.

1. The neoclassical theory is contradictory in saying that the actual concrete reality of God in inclusive of abstractions. Consider an abstract and necessary character of God, for instance, that at any time God must be supreme relative to what is in the world at that time. At any given time, this principle is instantiated in a particular way relative to what is in the world. But the principle itself is universal, and even an infinite number of instances of it would not constitute the reality of the universal principle, since they would only be particular instances and nothing intrinsically universal. No being who is an individual, growing through particular occasions, can contain the universality of a universal, only particular embodiments of it. If God has abstract elements it is only because God is a complex embodiment or instantiation of universal principles whose reality *as universal* is different from the divine self. That God is an *exemplification* of metaphysical principles Ogden admits.[29] Therefore it is contradictory to say that the concrete reality of God is the whole of which abstract universals are parts. The concrete reality is a whole of which *instances* of universals are parts (all the parts of particulars or actual things are particular or actual); the universals *per se* are something different. The universal always transcends the concrete.[30] Transcendent universals pose an embarrassment for neo-

classical metaphysics as we saw above in that those universals, such as the principle of supremacy, are transcendent of and *normative* for God; God, for instance, *must* be supreme. To expand the notion of God's reality to include the universal principles *per se* would be to deny God's particular temporal existence, or to make that temporal existence merely an abstract part of a trans-temporal or eternal whole.

2. A metaphysical theory ought to account for the unity of things. In what sense does God unify the particulars in the world? According to neoclassical metaphysics, and to the analogy of self and brain cells, God unifies the plurality of particulars by including them in divine knowledge, by prehending them together. But what God prehends is their objective realities, their realities for knowers. By definition, God cannot prehend their subjective realities in process of concrescence. The subjective process, just because it is a process of bringing a state of affairs to actuality, is not a datum to be known. Therefore, in themselves all the things in the world are external to God, unknowable by God. In Whitehead's language, an actual occasion can be an objective datum for another occasion's prehension only when it has subjectively perished. Considering things as they exist in themselves, according to process philosophy, all relations are external, not internal as Ogden claims; they are internal only when things are considered as objects for experience. If all relations are subjectively external, then neoclassical metaphysics has not accounted for the unity of things; certainly God cannot unify the world, since God can prehend the things in it only after their subjective reality or process has ceased to be.

This is a disastrous consequence for the religious applicability of the neoclassical concept of God since it means, in effect, that God knows only the objective reality of things, not the things themselves as subjects. This consequence might be avoided if the process understanding of the subjective reality of finite occasions were abjured. But if that were done all the cheers about temporality and creativity would be hollow, and the whole theory of God's sympathy would collapse. Accepting the consequence, it might be well to look again at those classical theories that, by reference to creation, account for how God is present to the subjective reality of things, "closer to them than they are themselves" as their creative ground. There is no contradiction in the claim that God creates a procession of processing actual occasions.

The fact that the neoclassical concept of God can include neither the normative universal principles that make God necessarily what he is relative to the world, nor the world considered in itself, makes the theory "radically incoherent," to throw back Ogden's description of classical theories. The attempt to combine abstract and universal necessity with concrete relatedness by the notion of dipolarity has difficulties just as grave as those Ogden imputes to classical theology.

IV

I have been obliged already to cast doubt on the claim that the neoclassical conception is especially helpful in solving the problem of the significance of life. And, quite contrary to the neoclassical claim, its view of God limits divine knowledge to mere data, not to the processing realities themselves.[31] Now I want to turn to the three problems Ogden deals with in detail, that of God's action in history, of the Lordship of Christ and of the Eschaton. Ogden argues in each case that neoclassical metaphysics is in a good position to make sense of the traditional Christian dogmatic doctrines. In general Ogden is refreshingly acute in seeing what is at the heart of the dogmatic problems, far more acute than most of the particular dogmatic traditions he examines. But I fear that here again his defense of neoclassical metaphysics fails.

1. Ogden agrees with Bultmann that God cannot act in history in a way that could properly be studied by science.[32] Still, it is religion's task, he says, to re-present God as creator and redeemer. What this means literally is the following. There is no event in the world that does not prehend both God and the antecedent world God had influenced; in this sense God can be called the *partial creator* of every event. Since each worldly event has its subjective reality as a process of bringing its prehensions to unity, each event is also partially self-created.[33] But God is the only creator whose influence is universal by necessity. God *redeems* in the sense that any event is prehended by God exactly as it is and is combined with the other divine prehensions in the best possible way; nothing if forgotten and everything is made the best of.

Now there are two senses in which a thing can act, according to
this neoclassical interpretation.[34] The vulgar sense is the external
influencings in which a thing engages. But the primary sense is the
internal process of constituting one's prehensions in a harmony
such that, when it is prehended by others, it has effects. True action therefore is internal; and in a literal sense external action is a
representation of inner action. God's inner action cannot be
called action in history in any ordinary sense, however. It is *universally* relevant to every event, whereas historical actions are
special. But since people interpret some events as more symbolic
than others, certain events can re-present God in a special way,
re-presenting universal divine creation and redemption through a
special event. This can be called God's action in history. Religion
organizes these special events to re-present God's universal inner
reality. I have two objections to this view of divine action.

The first, a philosophical objection, is that the theory of actual
occasions is hard pressed to account for historical action of any
sort. According to Whitehead, a person extended through time is
a society of actual occasions, unified by common reiterated patterns. How is there enough substantiality in the continuity that
the later occasions are responsible for what the earlier ones
started? The later occasions are heirs of the results, but not of the
historical responsibility of the earlier ones. God must be a society
of occasions since Ogden wants to emphasize divine temporality.

The second, a theological objection, is that more is usually
meant by God's historical action than Ogden tries to account for.
It is not that there is a universal goal that God works to bring
about by special symbolic events, but rather that God has a special goal that has meaning only in terms of its historical context.
So Christians claim that salvation consists in participation in
Jesus of Nazareth, the risen Christ, not that participation in Jesus
is historically symbolic of a historically universal salvation.
Perhaps everyone is saved; but this would be a historical contingency, not a metaphysical necessity. What this difficulty
illustrates is that Ogden's criticism of classical theology tells even
more against him. God's action relative to the world, for neoclassical metaphysics, is necessitated; there is metaphysical necessity
that God prehend everything perfectly (necessary redemption),
and that everything prehend divine influence (necessary crea-

tion). For those classical creation theories that put will prior to nature, creation and redemption are matters of grace, not necessity, and this is closer to the Christian experience, it seems to me. In classical Christianity, people thank God for gratuitous creation and salvation; for neoclassical Christianity, God cannot help but always do the best, and no thanks need be given. The chief wonder in the Christian experience is that divine grace which constitutes God as savior by bringing the world to participate in Christ when there is no antecedent necessity that God do so. Neoclassical metaphysics cannot escape necessitarianism.

2. In his essay, "What Does It Mean to Affirm 'Jesus Christ Is Lord'?," Ogden copes with the implication that Jesus is a re-presentation of the universal character of God.[35] Jesus is the one true re-presentation of the original ground of confidence in the significance of life, all other objects of ultimate loyalty being false gods; Jesus shows us what authentic life is in the light of God's creation and redemption. Ogden has an admirably subtle discussion of the problem of subordinationism at this point, recognizing it as the real problem of his Christology. He concludes in explication of St. Paul (I Cor. 8: 4–6) that God the Father, to whom Jesus the Lord is alleged to be subordinated unjustly, is really the God of Old Testament history, and that Jesus Christ is just a continuation of it. About Paul, Ogden says,

> In his view, the reality signified by the words, "God our Father" is, in the last analysis, one and the same with the reality designated as "our Lord Jesus Christ"—or better expressed, what it means to have God as our Father is existentially the same as having Jesus Christ as our Lord.[36]

Ogden's strategy is to interpret God the Father as a set of re-presentations, with which Christ is continuous. But in this case both the Father and the Son are subordinated to the real God; this is an incipient economic trinitarianism run wild. Besides, it is ambiguous how historical Ogden means the Old Testament Father God to be; it could be the real God as symbolized in Old Testament revelatory events—in which case Christ and the Old Testament symbols of the Father would be subordinated to the Father—or it could be an identification of the Father with the symbols themselves (e.g., the burning bush, the pillar of fire, etc.)—which seems idolatrous. At any rate, this hardly seems orthodox Christology, for whatever that is worth.

3. Ogden's eschatology is based on the splendid insight that the eschatological doctrines are primarily about God, not human beings.

> Like certain liberal theologians who insisted that "resurrection" has to do, not with the *quantity* of life, but with its *quality*, existentialists too easily obscure that the symbol's fundamental reference is to neither the quantity nor the quality of man's life, but to the quality of *God's* life—to the pure unbounded love, the perfect grace and judgement, whereby our creaturely lives in time are alone endowed with everlasting significance.[37]

Ogden defines love as God's action, "whereby, in each new present, he constitutes himself as God by participating fully and completely in the world of his creatures, thereby laying the ground for the next stage of the creative process."[38]

Participation means God's perfectly relative prehension and unsurpassable ordering of given prehensions that may in turn be prehended.[39] We suspect from our preceding discussion what Ogden can say now; our existential reality is constituted by a God who perfectly knows us and always sees us for the best.

> Because God's love, radically unlike ours, is pure and unbounded, and because he, therefore, both can and does participate fully in the being of all his creatures, the present moment for him never slips into the past as it does for us. . . . In other words, because God not only *affects*, but is also *affected by*, whatever exists, all things are in every present quite literally resurrected or restored in his own everlasting life, from which they can nevermore be cast out. . . . Faith knows that the final end or, as it were, the ultimate posterity of the whole creation is none other than God himself, who through his free decision in each moment to accept all things into his life overcomes the "perpetual perishing" of death and all its terrors.[40]

Because of its recognition that human life is necessarily and universally affected by God's love (participation), Ogden concludes that faith says in the last analysis "to God alone be the glory."[41]

Concerning sin Ogden says,

> Because faith is faith in a God whose love is without limit and who, therefore, accepts his creatures solely because of his own free decision to do so and not because or even in spite of them, faith also knows that the power of sin itself is finally broken by God's love. Or, better said, faith knows that not even man's sin can set a limit to God's free decision in each new present to love his creatures and give them to share in his own divine life.[42]

Several points of critical commentary are called for here.

To begin with, it is false on neoclassical grounds to say that God's love is unbounded: It is bounded by the limits of the objective reality of the things in the world. God cannot love things in their processive subjective reality because *that* cannot be prehended. What things are in themselves as opposed to what they are for subsequent occasions of experience does indeed slip into the past, perpetually perishing. According to Whitehead (whom Ogden seems to reject at this point), there is *only objective* immortality, and the loss through perpetual perishing of subjective reality is the ground of tragedy.[43]

Further, the merely objective presence of the world's events in the everlasting memory of God is not what Scripture means by resurrecton. If there is any analogue for eternal *life* in process philosophy, it is the subjective moment of creative process. This is true whether eternal life means a present state of affairs or a future one after death. The subjective moment of creative process is precisely what God cannot be present to or prehend in itself, on neoclassical grounds. Life in this sense is necessarily separation from God, not participation in God as Scripture would imply.

Also, Ogden simply has insufficient right to say, "to God alone be the glory." The final end or ultimate posterity of the whole creation on the neoclassical theory cannot be none other than God alone, but *must* include some other along with God. It is a metaphysical necessity, for the neoclassical view, that God have at every moment a world to prehend. True, God is the only being who perdures throughout infinite time; but there never is a moment when there is not a world of some being opposed to God. If there were not, God would have nothing to be relative to and would lose the concrete divine being. To give up the integrity of the world with its own inalienable subjective process would be to give up its autonomy and the ultimate significance that Ogden thinks secular people would like. What Ogden should say instead is "to God and some state of the world be the glory."

Scripture says that people's resurrection is a participation in Christ's resurrection, that "in Christ all shall be made alive" (I Cor. 15:22).[44] But if Christ is only a re-presentation, and if we truly participate in God who is known by neoclassical metaphysics, we cannot participate in Christ himself. Ogden rightly sees that he has to say that our resurrection is only *like* Christ's.

Moreover, it is misleading, on neoclassical grounds, for Ogden to say that God makes a free decision to accept his creatures. As noted before, God is necessitated to prehend accurately whatever the world presents. And if the doctrine of participation is in fact able to make sense of divine love, then by implication God's love is necessitated, and in no way can be called a free decision. On neoclassical grounds, there is nothing remarkable about the fact that, while we were yet sinners, God showed love for us with Christ's death (Rom. 5:8); although the historical Jesus might have run away, God could not help but love us.

Finally, just as God, conceived neoclassically, must share the glory with some state of the world, so the world can prevent the glory from being worth much (on Ogden's interpretation of glory). God must prehend people exactly as they are, necessarily loving them despite their sins, and always doing the best with them.[45] But, although God always makes the best of things, the things of which God makes the best may not allow the best to be very good. Since people maintain the integrity of their subjective reality over against God, and since for time everlasting some states of the nondivine universe must do this, a perverse world can everlastingly frustrate God's attempt to bring about much good. While the second coming of Christ to reign in glory may be mythology that should or should not be given a literal reconstruction, it seems clear that neoclassical theology cannot do it.[46]

The theme of this chapter has been that Ogden's version of neoclassical philosophy is not as good a candidate for a contemporary natural theology as it is sometimes represented.

Ogden however is not the only defender of the thesis that neoclassical philosophy is uniquely helpful to Christianity. Attention has been paid above to Charles Hartshorne himself; although he does not make Ogden's claims that his views are compatible with Christianity, he does claim with great sophistication that they are true. Furthermore, my general claim about neoclassical philosophy needs to be referred to John B. Cobb, Jr. The discussion of Cobb in Chapter Seven will extend the topic to his theory of world religions rather than Christianity alone. This discussion of Ogden will have to suffice for consideration of process theism as a specifically Christian philosophy. Meanwhile, Chapter Six will consider another view of process theology, namely, that it is positively continuous with the classical tradition by virtue of the mediation of transcendental theology, the legacy of Kant in Neothomism.

•VI•

Process Theism as
Transcendental Theology

Transcendental thought represents one approach to philosophical theology, process thought another. Despite the
vigorous and wise attempts of thinkers such as Schubert Ogden
to integrate the two, the approaches have remained largely dissociated in paideia, aim and personnel. Professor Charles Winquist
has contributed a significant essay with the purpose of showing
that certain aspects of Whitehead's speculative cosmology provide a model answering fundamental questions raised by the
transcendental theories of Kant, Marechal, Lonergan, Coreth and
Heidegger. Without doubt, this essay proves Winquist to be
among the small number of theological writers who think very
hard about the most important questions.[1] If his purpose is
achieved, Winquist has accomplished something splendid. If the
purpose is not achieved, his effort is of such excellence as to cast
doubt upon the felicity of the purpose itself.

Winquist's line of argument can be stated in a fairly neutral,
preliminary way. (1) In light of the pervasive secularization of
culture and language, philosophical theology ought to provide a
transcendental critique of theology, asking about the ontological
presuppositions of religious language, especially language about
transcendence. (2) The clue is Kant's transcendental imagination, which is associated with Lonergan's notion of insight connecting forms of thought with data. But, whereas Lonergan
believes reality must be proportional to the structure of knowing
it (a dialectical illusion as Winquist points out), the reality about
which religion speaks must be more fundamental. (3) The true
transcendental question is about the presupposition, not of the

structure of knowledge, but of the knowing act itself; the knowing act, or questioning act, is intimately associated with transcendental imagination. (4) The structure of transcendental imagination is best explained by Whitehead's cosmology of concrescent actual occasions.

I

Winquist, along with Ogden, is surely correct that contemporary theology must pitch its tent in contemporary secular culture. The authority of any intellectual language, such as theology, derives ultimately from its being able to enlighten and enhance the culture of the people who use it. But religion does not play a large role in secular culture. In fact, the role allotted to religion too often turns out to be the fulfillment of some secular task—teaching morals, promoting causes such as civil rights, etc.—and not the articulation of a stance toward transcendence or something absolute. Winquist states clearly that the question of transcendence is the proper one for philosophical theology, and thereby provides a critical edge lacking in Ogden.

The move to transcendental philosophy is not an innocent one, however, in the context of the apparent triumph of secularism. Winquist's own words are important for seeing his project properly.

> We need a philosophical theology which is not concerned with the construction of a contemporary natural theology, but which is committed to the task of providing a transcendental critique of theology. This critique will seek to disclose the ontological ground and the ontological meaning of doing theology. The philosophical theologian must construct a transcendental philosophy which will provide principles which are regulative of the scope and significance of the act of theological understanding but which are not determinative of the content of that understanding. It would be a mistake for the philosophical theologian to try to substitute philosophical concepts for theological concepts in the development of a systematic theology when the question which he asks is about the possibility and not the content of theology.[2]

In a general sense, a transcendental inquiry is concerned with uncovering the formal presuppositions of some actual experiential content. Kant's question was how to account for the possibility of a priori knowledge in science and mathematics. If something is actual, it must be possible: What are the transcendental conditions of its possibility? Therefore, whereas transcendental philosophy asks about "the possibility and not the content of theology," *it must presuppose the content of theology* just as Kant must presuppose that there exists some a priori knowledge.

But a secular society is precisely one in which religious experience and language—the relevant content for Winquist's enterprise—is suspect, doubtful, or even absent. To ask about the presuppositions of a doubtful beginning can give rise to no more than doubtful presuppositions; from the standpoint of the secular person, the presuppositions of an illusion are either sham (Ayer, *et al.*) or pathology (Freud). To show how theology could be possible *if it is not an illusion* is hardly to advance.

This is why many process theologians do not find the transcendental tradition a promising strategy. I myself agree with John Cobb and others who prefer a more frontal assault on secular intellectual suppositions by constructing a "contemporary natural theology," plus an insistence that secular experience is not the only valid kind today.[3]

But suppose we undertake the transcendental strategy nevertheless; after all, some of the most profound intellectual resources are to be found in that tradition. Where do we stand with respect to the dilemma that contemporary secular experience does not have the certified content from which a transcendental argument can be launched?

One move would be to adopt the intellectual apparatus of an age when religious experience and language were felt to be well grounded. In a sense, Winquist's use of neoscholasticism reflects this move; that tradition has a pre-Cartesian confidence that the root of human intellect is surely relevant to the nature of things. But, although Winquist makes copious use of neoscholastic terminology, he generally does not lose sight of its limits.

Another move would be to find one's certified content in areas of contemporary experience that are not as secular as they seem to be. Religion professors who talk about embracing secularism may always be suspected of a secret participation in nonsecular experience. A genuinely secular person would not worry about transcendence at all. It is clear from Winquist's book that the experiences crucial to his thinking are not secular ones. He has just the right formula in response: "The theologian sacrifices a responsiveness to the wholeness of man if he uncritically adopts secularism, and yet his work is irrelevant if he ignores the presence of secularism in our culture."[4] The question to be raised, however, is where to pay attention to secularism. Should secularism set the conditions for the respectability of theology? If not (as I think), then transcendental philosophy and concern for language lose much of their attractiveness as apologetic devices. Of course, understanding their own presuppositions is a proper concern for the theologians themselves; but for them there should be less interest in discovering the possibility of theology *without the content* than in interpreting the content of theology with attention paid to the logical structure of its possibility. If it be argued that the content of theology is dogmatic and only the form is philosophical, then one should read beyond Kant to Hegel; the distinction between form and content is far more problematic than Winquist observes. Although there are times when Winquist in *The Transcendental Imagination* seems to forget that secularism is a problem, by and large he does not appeal to extrasecular religious experience with which to begin his transcendental argument.[5]

Winquist's basic move is similar to Tillich's. Pure secularity is not a genuine option. Just as Tillich said that everyone has an ultimate concern (and that makes one religious no matter how bad the religion), Winquist says that everyone must be open to questioning the presuppositions of questioning transcendence itself. This is so by nature of the structure of reason, and it is quite irrelevant whether secular people ever get around to such questioning.

> Our starting point is very simple, the questionability of existence which cannot be questioned without contradiction. . . . As a transcendental condition of questioning, we can affirm that man is an entity whose being is a being directed toward being. . . . What is the existential significance of the act of knowing? This is the starting point for an ontology.[6]

The root of Winquist's transcendental argument is that man's nature as a questioning being has presuppositions providing the
transcendental form of philosophical theology. Is this a solid
foundation? Ayer would say it is nonsense, and Freud called it
pathological except for adolescents. Let us consider the argument
in detail.

II

Winquist begins his discussion of the transcendental imagination with Kant. He interprets Kant to say that, *if* any judgment is
universal or necessary, then it is apriori (my emphasis, not his).
He briefly traces Kant's discussion of the apriori forms of sensibility and the apriori categories, both of which Kant claims are
necessary to account for apriori synthetic knowledge in science
and mathematics. (Winquist neglects to emphasize that the
apriori status of the forms of sensibility and the categories are dependent on the prior acceptance of the apriori status of certain
propositions in mathematics and science.) Because the forms of
sensibility and the categories must be integrated in any knowledge whose content is given through intuition but which must be
thought through categories of the understanding, Kant's schematism of the transcendental imagination is the crux of the issue.
The schematism, which consists of the rules for constructing
images of concepts within the form of time (and sometimes
space), provides what Winquist, following Lonergan, calls
"heuristic structures" constituting apriori knowledge of the
world.

> We are using the term *heuristic* because the transcendental imagina-
> tion brings to an insight a form to be filled; and, while prescinding
> from the empirical content which will fill the form, it works out the
> procedure defining the general properties of schemata which are the
> conditions for being-in-the-world.[7]

At this point Winquist suggests he has made a good start, having
yet only to determine what the apriori conditions are and whether
they apply to knowledge alone or to being.

But notice! The truth of Kant's theory has not been argued *but merely assumed.* We may grant that, *if* there is any universal or necessary knowledge, it is apriori. We may also grant that, *if* there is any apriori knowledge, it consists in the knowledge of transcendental conditions of experience. But Winquist believes that the possibility that there are transcendental conditions of experience proves that experience is in fact transcendentally conditioned and that there is apriori knowledge. This simply does not follow. There is no reason to buy the transcendental model, to believe that space and time are apriori conditions of sensibility, to believe that any concepts of understanding are apriori categories, unless there is some bona fide apriori synthetic knowledge requiring them for its possibility. This is a flagrant begging of the question of the truth of the transcendental approach.

Let me try to make clear what is at stake here. The transcendental claim is that the conditions for experience, those heuristic structures, are sources of apriori knowledge in a very strict sense. As Winquist will argue, when we get them straight they provide ontological knowledge that underlies any ontic knowledge for which they are enabling conditions. Kant, in the *Critique of Pure Reason* B2, distinguished this strict sense of apriori from a looser sense in which an empirical generalization from experience might provide "apriori" expectations regarding particular cases; in the latter sense one, for instance, should know "apriori" (that is, from generalized past experience) that if one undermines one's house it will fall down. Now a nontranscendental cosmologist, such as a process philosopher, might very well allow that there are universal conditions of experience, for instance, space and time, some categories, or Whitehead's categoreal obligations. But these would not be strictly apriori in a transcendental philosophical sense; they would be empirical generalizations, or parts of a speculative hypothesis which is an empirical generalization considered as a whole. For a speculative cosmologist such as Peirce or Whitehead, whether such and such are universal or necessary judgments regarding experience is an empirical matter. This would not make sense in the logic of transcendental philosophy. Transcendental philosophy gains its plausibility from having to account for knowledge already accepted to be apriori and synthetic. Nontranscendental philosophy has no need to find such knowledge. It is clear that Winquist (with Kant, Lonergan and

Heidegger) does not want a mere speculative hypothesis about the way we know, but real knowledge of what knowledge (and being) must be.

Winquist astutely notes that not many people are satisfied today with Kant's forms and categories. He does not, however, ask whether this is because we no longer believe that science and mathematics (or religion or anything else) exhibit synthetic apriori judgments. He asks, rather, whether the transcendental conditions Kant specified—the forms of sensibility, the categories, the schematic principles and so forth—are the correct ones. He answers that these are "classical" heuristic structures and that we know now that probability or statistical heuristic structures are needed.

> A statistical investigation is an attempt to give intelligibility to a coincidental manifold that exists in the empirical residue left from an investigation using classical heuristic structures. Statistical heuristic structures also give a synthetic unity to the transcendental imagination, but they do so by grounding the "I think" in the notion of an emergent probability.... The notion of probability belongs to a transcendental aesthetic and the principles that it imposes upon our experience of being-in-the-world to a transcendental deduction. The fact that probability can be a sufficient formal condition for the unity of an insight leads us to a broadened conception of the transcendental imagination.[8]

We may ask at this point whether the nature of probability is not itself a synthetic apriori bit of knowledge replacing Kant's unfortunate belief in the exclusive validity of Euclidian geometry, etc. It can be argued, for instance, that the very meaning of a speculative hypothesis as a philosophic alternative to transcendental claims presupposes a notion of probability. Does not the meaning of hypothesis presuppose a view regarding its verification? Of course there is some such presupposition. But the theory of probability or verification and of the hypothetical nature of the speculative hypothesis is only a higher level theory than that in the contents of the speculative hypothesis. A change in the content of the speculative hypothesis, occasioned perhaps by new discoveries in physics or biology or religion, might entail a change in the higher level theory about hypotheses and probability. That is, the validity of probability theory as a condition for knowing the world should be seen to rest on evidence of its applicability and adequacy, not on a transcendental argument that is apriori and beyond the test of evidence.

The conclusion at this stage in the argument is that Winquist, like a great many before him, has failed to justify the transcendental elements of his argument. Nothing has been shown to be apriori. The universality or necessity of statistical structures as unifying conditions of experience is at best true as an empirical generalization on a high level. For myself, then, the argument from here on should be construed as a plain speculative hypothesis, dialectically argued.

But suppose we accept Winquist's use of Kant at face value. Where does he go from here? He raises the question of the difference between the structures of knowing and the structures of being. Can we say that reality itself has structures proportionate to the structures of knowledge according to which reality can be known? Even if we could, there would be no point to it unless we could also say that reality's structures are independent or transcendent of the cognitive context; as Kant argued, this is impossible. But, following Maréchal and Lonergan, Winquist argues that the proportionality between objective reality and knowledge should be sought with the knowledge pole represented by the dynamic act of knowing rather than by the structure of the content of knowledge. They assert that there is a pure desire to know supposed in all cognitive acts, although not perfectly satisfied by any. The dynamic thrust of this act, according to Marechal and Lonergan, entails a transcendent reality that would satisfy the conditions of complete knowledge. Because no finite phenomenal knowledge logically could satisfy the unrestricted striving of finite acts of cognition, the conditions for the intelligibility of the knowing act entail that reality be completely intelligible. "The real as completely intelligible is identical with the notion of being which is defined as the complete set of answers to the complete set of questions."[9] Therefore, according to Lonergan, transcendental understanding of the act of knowing—and the affirmation of self involved—entails affirming that there is a transcendent reality, the natural finality toward which intellect tends.

Winquist correctly points out that this data is dialectical illusion, in Kant's terms. The very meaning of the *Critique of Pure Reason* is that it is illusory to infer from what would fulfill the demands of reason for completeness to a reality fulfilling those demands. Given this very basic criticism, so clearly seen, I am not sure why Winquist bothers as much as he does with Lonergan. But he takes him to have contributed the insight that we should look at the act of knowing rather than at the content. The reason for Lonergan's failure to transcend dialectical illusion, according to Winquist, is that he limits his considerations to epistemology, explicitly rejecting metaphysics. Winquist's own strategy is to move to a metaphysics or ontology of the knowing act. But is that not simply an abandonment of the transcendental approach?

III

"A transcendental analysis of the *act* of knowing asks the question as to what the structures of being are which make knowing possible."[10] The force of the word *transcendental* in that sentence is that the analysis will produce not a speculative theory about how knowing is a possible kind of being, but a deduction of what being must be if real knowledge is to be possible. But how do we know there is any real knowing, that is, knowledge that is not mere hypothesis more or less plausibly accepted? This is analogous to the question whether there is any actual synthetic apriori knowledge that serves as a starting point for an epistemological transcendental argument.

Winquist answers:

By calling into question the question about a starting point, we have affirmed the questionability of existence and we have established a horizon under which our reflections can take place. It would be contradictory to question the possibility of questioning. This unconditional act provides the initial possibility for the construction of an ontology of knowing.... As far as our search for a beginning is concerned, the asking of the question as a starting point for ontology has made available for philosophical inquiry a concrete experience to be used in locating the transcendental conditions necessary for questioning itself. My intention is to show that the transcendental conditions for questioning form a horizon under which we can then seek to determine the ontological structures of knowing in general.[11]

Before this position is examined, it is important to point out that the extremely intellectualist cast of the above quotation and of all Winquist's argument in this area is not typical. Beginning with his criticism of Kant and Lonergan, Winquist steadily urges that cognitive acts should be considered much more broadly than those modeled on intellectual assertions. He suggests consideration of dreams, the subconscious, the hallucinations of drunkenness or drugs, mysticism and so forth. But the intellectual model is apparently the cleanest to work with.

The underpinning of Winquist's argument, as pointed out in the first section of this chapter, is the claim that to question existence is to provide an instance of the cognitive existence to be investigated. The questioning of existence proves that ontology does have a real subject matter and that it is an intellectual process that can only be done well or poorly, but not ignored. I suppose Winquist would say that even the secular person who doubts transcendence trucks with transcendence in the very doubting.

This bears a superficial resemblance to Descartes's argument that his existence is affirmed in his thinking; there is an even greater resemblance to Augustine's affirmation of his existence in his very doubting of it. But the resemblance is still only superficial. If I understand what is at stake in Winquist's argument, he is not concerned to prove a mere uninterpreted existence, but an existential cognitive act of a certain normative sort. That is, the questioning of existence could not be metaphysical nonsense or adolescent psychopathology; it is a real engagement with being. Winquist would move from this point to an interpretation of what kind of engagement this is and call upon Heidegger's theory of *Dasein* to say what kind of being a person must be in order to question existence.

That the questioning of existence engages being *is a theory*, however, not a self-evident starting point for ontology. To assert it as the latter begs the question of transcendental ontology. The experience of questioning existence is also explainable by the positivist theory that people speak a lot of nonsense and, by the

Freudian theory that adolescents are driven to employ certain il-
lusions to handle problems of their development at that stage, or
by a host of other theories representing it as a contingent part of
some lives. Now the belief that questioning existence is essential
to human life as such may be *a better theory than the others.* I
believe it is, within certain limits. *But it is a theory nevertheless,
not a transcendental element.* Of course any serious and meaningful questioning of existence is by definition the real thing. But,
as Freud and others have pointed out, what we seem to be serious
about sometimes is not the real agenda; and, as the positivists
said, if people were not inclined to believe mistakenly that meaningless thought is meaningful, no one would ever engage in it.
The point is that whether or not existential questioning is genuine engagement with reality depends on whether the theory interpreting it as such is better than theories explaining it away as
something else. The problem is to probate theories, not to find a
transcendental starting point.

At this point in Winquist's argument, it seems to me, transcendental claims become irrelevant. Winquist employs a discussion
of Heidegger to develop a model of people as beings whose very
essence as beings involves questioning their existence. This
model is in fact treated as a speculative hypothesis, congruent
with and complemented by Whitehead's. But Winquist argues
from it as if he has to some extent proved the model, showing it to
be a transcendental condition of questioning. This he has not
done. Nevertheless, just to present a speculative hypothesis as
complex as this one is to make an advance, and Winquist's
achievement here is important.

From Heidegger he derives two main requirements for the
model. The first is that human beings be conceived as involved in
internal relations with what they know, including being. The second is that the model interpret what Heidegger calls "throwness," an historical or "factical" contingency connected with the
centrality of time for inner sense. But, whereas Heidegger sees
time as central and almost exclusive as a heuristic structure, Winquist wants to expand the notion.

> In seeking a unity for the act of knowing we have again returned
> to the notion of the transcendental imagination. We have finally af-

firmed that the being of the *act* of knowing is determined by the heuristic structures of the transcendental imagination. Thus, an analysis of *Dasein* finds its unity in the heuristic structures of the transcendental imagination. We part with Heidegger because of his suggestion that temporality is the single determination of the unity of the transcendental imagination.

We need a new set of categories to understand the ontological conception of the transcendental imagination implied in a shift from the exclusive use of classical heuristic methods to the complementary use of classical and nonclassical heuristic methods. However, we must continue to try to develop a fundamental ontology because that which we are seeking is present to us in that which we are.[12]

But Winquist has not established that what "we are seeking is present to us in that which we are." Therefore, there is no justification here for fundamental ontology as a transcendental discipline. This is not to keep us from a speculative hypothetical ontology, however, which is where Winquist next takes us.

IV

The most helpful model of human being-in-the-world is Whitehead's, Winquist suggests. He shows how Whitehead would interpret internal relations (the doctrine of prehension) and "throwness" (the subjective aim derivative from God that transcends the nexuses prehended in the actual world of the occasion). Transcendental imagination becomes the process of concrescence combining physical and conceptual prehensions according to propositions luring the occasion on to greater order and value. Those luring propositions, derivative from the initial subjective aim, ultimately from the transcendent primordial nature of God, are the long sought heuristic principles.

What Winquist has effected is a brilliant translation of the problems of transcendental theology into the naturalistic standpoint of Whitehead's conceptual scheme. Whatever complaints I may have about the content of Whitehead's system, I would agree that as a cosmology its articulateness and detail are a great advance on the transcendental philosophies interpreted as speculative cosmologies or ontologies. Rather than enter into discussion of the wisdom of Winquist's interpretation of Whitehead at the points of the usual scholarly controversies, I want to consider a problem he rightly sees to be central to his enterprise.

The transcendental tradition from the beginning has seen human cognition, however broadly that is interpreted, as essential to the nature of man. The act of knowing is the strategic element for Winquist's main argument. Heidegger goes so far as to suggest that "language is the way that man comes into the world and stands as a historical reality."[13] Yet Whitehead believed that consciousness and human knowledge are only the tip of the iceberg of concrescence—rare, sophisticated and fleeting occurrences in the world's process. Furthermore, he believed that philosophers often get into trouble by paying too much attention to language. The subject-predicate structure of language gives misleading plausibility to substance philosophies. Does this disagreement over the importance and philosophical use of language pose serious problems for Winquist's marriage of transcendental and process philosophies?

In one sense, the problem is merely semantic. Whitehead would agree that human life in distinction from lower forms emerges only with the emergence of language. Higher experience requires language. Winquist quotes *Modes of Thought*:

> The mentality of mankind and the language of mankind created each other. If we like to assume the rise of language as a given fact, then it is not going too far to say that the souls of men are the gift from language to mankind.
>
> The account of the sixth day should be written, He gave them speech, and they became souls.[14]

Furthermore, Whitehead's analysis of the lower elements of experience in concrescence can easily be translated into metaphors about language. The metaphysical conception of "proposition" is already a start in that direction. Heidegger would be just as wary as Whitehead about using the structure of language as a model for the world; the Heideggerian concern for language focuses on its use in poetry when its structure is transcended. Winquist very nicely spells out these reconciliations.

In another sense, however, the problem is far deeper. Whitehead was a cosmologist, a philosopher of nature. Mankind, for him, with its language and characteristic higher experiences, is emergent from lesser forms through a process seeking the realization of even finer values. The function of philosophy is to understand this natural process with all its components, including God and human civilization. Of course, philosophical understanding is one of the higher experiences of which only higher forms are capable. But this is not an especially significant truth; it is what we would expect from the process conception of levels of nature.

For Heidegger, however, the special kind of knowledge in which being is a problem for people is central for the constitution of the world as such. From the transcendental perspective, the world is possible only because of the conditions for essential human knowing. The point is not that philosophy is possible only when there are human beings, that philosophical knowledge is human knowledge, that the world is known according to the limits of human knowledge—with all of this Whitehead would agree. The Heideggerian point is that the heuristic structures of the most profound human knowledge are the conditions for the meaningfulness of speaking of a world at all. If the move from epistemology to ontology is made, those heuristic structures are not only the conditions for knowing, but the ontological conditions for being.

In his move to Whitehead, Winquist has naturalized the transcendental standpoint. The heuristic structures found in Whitehead's scheme are not those especially revealed in people's existence as questioners of their own existence. In the process of concrescence they are just as well exhibited in a mouse or an electron. And Whitehead would probably prefer to analyze them in simpler kinds of occasions, precisely because the complication of them required for higher human experience would likely obscure what is essential. For Whitehead, persons questioning their existence are highly complex versions of simpler entities; the greater complexity gives rise to vast and all-important differences in quality, but there is a continuum of nature. For Heidegger, by contrast, the mouse and the electron depend for their existence on the constitutive human heuristic principles; in a sense *Dasein* is the antecedent condition for electrons and mice.

Whitehead would like to limit the importance of language in

philosophy because of its tendency to suggest anthropomorphic mistakes: Lower forms will be read as if they were higher ones, thereby neglecting the qualitative changes in process. Heidegger must insist on the philosophical importance of language because it is only through the existential stretching of language that people can attain to their authentic existence; authentic human existence is the condition for there being a world. Unsympathetic Heideggerians will think Winquist has sold the transcendental birthright for a mess of process pottage.

V

Winquist writes:

> If we accept Tillich's demand that theology be responsive to the existential realities of the situation in which it is present, then because of our affirmation that language is an ontological element constitutive of man's being in its passage into historical reality, we must also realize that a proper concern of theology is the meaning and interpretation of language.[15]

This project might mean two different things. For a Heideggerian it would mean a redefinition of theology to include "fundamental ontology." For a Whiteheadian it is a simple confusion of theology with anthropology; anthropology is the study of how language and its interpretation contribute to humanities; theology is the study of God and of the ways divinity bears particularly on the world and mankind. Of course, theologians must attend to problems of interpretation; this is an existential problem of great weight because Whitehead would agree with the hermeneutical tradition that proper interpretation requires a fundamental openness and perhaps a profound change in the interpreter. But hermeneutics is no more important for theologians than it is for philosophers, historians, artists or scientists.

The other side of the coin is that many things besides the interpretation of language in the theological sense contribute to the passage of mankind's being into historical reality. Any profound experience with truth, with freedom, with creativity, or with love is constitutive of the historical character of the higher phases of human experience.

The Heideggerian would answer that this view of hermeneutics ignores the distinction between the ontological and the ontic; it construes hermeneutical experiences as mere ontic developments. Indeed it does. For process philosophy, the heuristic structures laying out the ontological level are clearer in mice and electrons than in people. Of course only creatures with higher experience can *know* the ontological level; but they are not knowing their *knowledge* particularly. To use the distinction between the ontological and ontic levels for the description of process cosmology, the ontic level is far more important than the ontological for interpreting the subtle and highly valuable peculiarities of higher human experience, such as questioning existence as such. The existential act of doing ontology is an ontic achievement. Electrons and mice are ontologically real, exhibiting the heuristic structures in their being.

My first conclusion from this discussion is that, if one complements Heidegger with Whitehead, one's theology need not give an especially central place to hermeneutics. More central to a Whiteheadian theology are metaphysical cosmology and empirical history as sources of general and special revelation. But if one does want to make hermeneutics central as a theological concern, then it is crucial to preserve the transcendental standpoint from a Whiteheadian naturalization that would make mice and electrons proper hermeneutical agents. Winquist believes he has sustained the transcendental standpoint; I think he is mistaken.

A second conclusion generalizes the first. Winquist has reconciled the transcendental tradition with process thought only by undermining what is essential and distinctive to the former. Contrary to his intention, he has not provided a transcendental critique of theology but instead has given a naturalistic Whiteheadian interpretation of the central transcendental concept, the transcendental imagination. Now in my own view this is a fine thing. The transcendental contributions to philosophy and theology are worth most when naturalized, it seems to me. But thinkers in the transcendental tradition would not agree, and we should be plain about the costs of this reconciliation.

A third conclusion is that, despite his heroic attempt at integral synthetic philosophical theology, Winquist's argument remains eclectic. But, in an important sense, it accurately reflects our theological situation: Despite the best wits of our most sympathetic theologians and philosophers, the diverse theological traditions cannot be reconciled on the most profound matters of program. This is not Winquist's fault.

A last conclusion is that the transcendental tradition in theology is largely wrong. If we indeed live in a secular era, then there can be no transcendental critique of theology because theology itself is suspect. To assert that genuine existential questioning proves there is a real transcendent object, even when the assertion is bolstered by a dialectical interpretation of the dynamic act of knowing, is a dialectical illusion in Kant's sense. To ask the fundamental existential question, to face one's foundations and historical throwness as *Dasein*, is a great human achievement; but to understand it transcendentally is no advance if a simpler ontic or cosmological understanding will do. A hermeneutical emphasis in theology is likely to anthropomorphize God needlessly, just as a hermeneutical emphasis in science would anthropomorphize mice and electrons. I fear that Winquist's main analysis of Whitehead is so fine that it makes the earlier discussions of Kant, Lonergan and Heidegger not only pointless but obfuscatory. Contrary to what Winquist said (in the first quotation from his essay, above), the possibility of philosophical theology is not half so interesting as its metaphysical and empirical content. Hegel criticized Kant for trying to understand what thought can do without trying it out. Hegel was right.

VI

The general topic of this chapter and the previous one has been an examination of the claim that process theology is superior to other theological approaches in providing a theoretical interpretation of religion. The previous chapter considered Shubert Ogden's view that process theology stands in contrast to classical Western theology and is superior because more cogent to contemporary secular culture. Whereas I agreed that it is absolutely crucial to be cogent in contemporary terms, I argued that Ogden's position was not always in a better position than that which he attacked.

Winquist's strategy in one sense has been the opposite of Ogden's. Rather than setting process theology off over against a rival, he has tried to demonstrate its continuity with transcendental philosophy, which in turn is a continuous development from classic medieval positions. But I have argued that process philosophy is fundamentally alien to the transcendental turn. In fact, it is closer to certain pretranscendental modes of thought than to twentieth-century transcendental theologians such as Marechal and Lonergan. Winquist's book provides yet one more demonstration of the preferability of process philosophy's naturalism to the apriori claims of transcendental thought. But if process philosophy's theological component carries with it as many difficulties as the previous chapters have argued, then it seems plausible now, from one more angle, to attempt to separate process cosmology and metaphysics from its theological component.

Before drawing that general conclusion, however, one more attempt to show the power of process theism for interpreting religion should be examined. John B. Cobb, Jr., not only has developed his own carefully reasoned version of the speculative categories defining process theology, but he has used it to form a perspective on world religions. If both Ogden and Winquist are correct in assessing the importance of making philosophical theology relevant to the contemporary situation, as I believe they are, then the experiential reference point for that theology is world religions, not just the Christian background of most of those who happen to be interested in theology.

·VII·

Process, Existence,
and World Religions

The encounter of Christianity with the world's religions is an event of great importance in the twentieth century. Shockwaves have been registered in all the traditions involved in the encounter. Since process theology has arisen out of the Western, primarily Christian, tradition it is important to assess its contributions to the encounter and to register the effects of the encounter on its own development. Whereas the previous chapters have focused on the conceptual structure of process theism, with appeals to experience made peripherally as "intuitions of the religious sensibility," the question of the structure of experience itself will now be focused upon as an object of disciplined inquiry. It was simple enough in Chapter One to conjure with the relativity of conceptual schemes by contrasting process theology's with another. The relativity of basic structures of traditional experience is far more difficult to handle without abandoning experience as a touchstone for thinking.

Process philosophy in general has been a fruitful conceptual tool for building bridges between Asian and Western cultures. Few thinkers have interpreted and guided this encounter within the area of religion with the universal sympathy, clarity and originality of John Cobb. These virtues are apparent and polished in his most significant book, *The Structure of Christian Existence.* An examination of that book provides access for considering the question of experience within process theology.

I

Cobb's analysis begins with the emergence in history of "axial" human beings from their primitive forebears.[1] Preaxial people took the unifying principles of their life from unconscious elements and thus are best understood in terms of their myths, the projections of their unconscious. The evolution of axial people, which took place in China, India, Persia, Greece and Israel in the 1000 years before the Common Era, involved the development of centers of experience organized in the reflective consciousness rather than in the unconscious. These new "seats of experience" struggled in various ways to gain power over the other elements of experience, and different cultures developed different structures of existence accordingly. Cobb details a one-two line of development for India, Greece and Israel.

In pre-Buddhistic India, according to Cobb, the centering of experience in consciousness brought to focus an awareness of the suffering of an endless, meaningless round of life; the structure of axial existence which developed, therefore, involved perfecting a distinction between the phenomenal world of change and the ontologically more real world of the unchanging self. Buddhism, particularly in its Mahayana forms, pushed a step farther in declaring the transcendent world of the self to be unreal and empty; although personal virtue consists in compassion for the plight of all, peace consists in extinguishing the desire for surmounting the plight.

In Homeric Greece, the structure of existence for axial people took the form of aesthetic distance from an objective world, enjoying the world for its formed character apart from desire and mythic projection. The development of the Socratic mentality, according to Cobb, made reason the seat of existence, objectifying aesthetic distance and adding a dialectical critical motif to people's relation to the objective world.

The structure of existence for the ancient Hebrews was that of the prophetic mentality, for whom something like the modern notion of the person took predominance over momentary existence as well as aesthetic feeling and rational distance. A "person," in the prophetic sense, is one who takes responsibility for actions, objectifying perception and reason. The seat of existence

for a "person" may be called will; the emphasis on voluntary definition of human life is closely connected with persons' definition
of themselves over against a God who makes contracts with
promises to keep and a morality to be obeyed. From the prophetic
came the "spiritual" person, the Christian structure of existence.
The crucial threshold to cross is objectifying the will itself and
taking responsibility for one's very feelings. Spiritual persons are
those who are concerned not only to do what is right, but to have
a right heart motivating their impulses. Adultery for Jesus was
not a matter of what one did but of what one wants to do, even if
the impulse is inhibited. The spiritual structure of existence involves an indefinite process of self-transcendence, whereby any
stage of development is itself objectified and made the subject of
personal responsibility.

This brief description of Cobb's thesis overschematizes his
subtle and nuanced account, but it gives the general rationale for
his historical conclusion. The Greek structures of existence have
been incorporated, albeit in subordinte positions, into the He-
braic-Christian structure, forming the Western tradition. The
great alternatives today, therefore, are Christianity in its developed form and Buddhism. (Cobb copes more subtly than I have
represented here with the problem of the earlier stages—Hinduism, Homeric Greece and Judaism—resisting absorption into the
later stages.) Modern people are faced with a choice between
Christianity and Buddhism as structures of existence with which
to start. Cobb emphasizes that this is a genuine choice between
options that are to all appearances irreconcilable.

> Both historically and systematically, the relation of spiritual exis-
> tence to Indian existence is radically different from its relation to
> either personal or Socratic existence. In the case of both personal
> and Socratic existence, consciousness, selfhood, and the power of
> the soul to transcend and to act upon its world were prized. Spiritual
> existence carried farther in the same direction a development al-
> ready affirmed and far advanced. Thus we can speak of fulfillment as
> well as transcendence or transformation of existing structures. But
> the Indian sages of the axial period had opposed this whole line of
> psychic development. To them it was essential either to establish the
> self beyond the differentiated world, which included the flow of
> psychic experience, or to annihilate selfhood altogether. Spiritual

existence is not the fulfillment of this effort. Nor can the Christian recognize in extinction of his self-transcending selfhood the fulfillment of his existence. Finally, it is impossible to conceive a third structure in which both spiritual selfhood and the extinction of self could be subsumed in some higher synthesis. Buddhism, as the culminating achievement of India, lies side by side with Christianity as an alternative mode of human realization. It stands as the ultimate challenge and limit to the Christian claim to finality.[2]

II

The bottom-line question on all this analysis is, finally, what choice to make. This is the question of finality. Cobb astutely warns against choosing on the basis of some rational value system, because that value system inevitably will reflect the perspective of one of the principal contending structures of existence. Of course Buddhism is deficient in accounting for history and the fulfillment of the concrete person, he says. And Christianity is deficient, from the Buddhist perspective, in that its ideal of Christ's love is impossible for this world and itself contributes to the suffering that should be avoided in compassionate emptiness.

Cobb's own argument takes the general form of saying that Christianity appears from the present point of view to have a more fruitful survival value in the face of technological advance and ecological threat. Particularly, because the underlying values of Western technology are winning the world, the importance of personal fulfillment will come to dominate worldwide passions. In another essay, "A New Christian Existence," Cobb deals at greater length with needed developments of Christianity to make it more fit for a genuinely worthwhile structure of existence.[3]

My own view is that the problem of finality is incompletely stated here, however elegantly Cobb has delineated its many parts. The model of choice between exclusive options is unrealistic. Perhaps Cobb's attraction to it reflects a legacy of Barth's God's thrown stone, somewhat surprising in Cobb's liberal tradition. A better model, one more natural for a Whiteheadian in fact, is to conceive contemporary people as seeking to weave a position for themselves from and within the wider environment of uninte-

grated resources. The diverse histories of the different traditional
resources in our world make them mutually incompatible in
many respects as they stand. But so are the givens for any occasion of existence, in the Whiteheadian sense. Taking up a present
position requires selecting from among the resources and appropriating them in compatible ways. The free choice comes in the
selection and emphasis given to a multitude of resources, not to
the wholesale adoption or rejection of complete environments.
Yet the latter is what seems to be implied by Cobb's model.

Most of the people in the world today, it seems to me, are in the
problematic situation of having to make for themselves new
structures of existence. For Christians the Christian resources are
closer to them and more easily integratable with the rest of their
environment than non-Western resources. In a Whiteheadian
analogy, the past occasions of our body are closer to us than those
of someone else's body. But the cultural resources of structures of
existence are *mental* entities, prehended by "hybrid physical
prehensions," to use Whitehead's term; far more than past body
states they are malleable and combinable with what appear to be
their contraries. It is easier to adopt some of the mental resources
of Yoga than the body postures, because they can be adopted in
small doses and in transformed ways: In sitting, you either get
both feet on your thighs or you do not. Easterners will find it easier to employ Eastern structures of existence, and Westerners the
opposite; but each can appropriate something of the resources of
the other.

What I am suggesting is that we are in a situation, worldwide,
of constructing new structures of existence, employing the old
diverse structures as data to be selected, weighed and harmonized. The new structures will be punctuated in different ways by
people from different traditions. Whether they will bear the name
of one or several of the old structures depends partly on such adventitious factors of who writes the histories, and partly on real
elements of relative dominance. The criteria guiding the development of this new structure of existence are those guiding any
creative effort: preserve as much as possible of the achieved richness of the past; attend to enriching the relevant present and future environment as much as adaptively possible; make the
environment more stable and supportive of the higher human

values, and make those higher human values contain the richest intensities of experience possible; respect the historical idiosyncrasies of individual choices.

III

Cobb's reading of the historical situation and mine each are hypotheses. Probation of the hypotheses stands logically (though perhaps not existentially) prior to the choice between structures of existence. But how does one test the hypotheses against each other? That they are both readings of the historical situation means that tests must be empirical in some sense. But the tests are not simply the discovery of more facts. Rather, they have to do with the interpretation of the facts, and the debatable factors in interpretation have more to do with models in this case than simply with facts.

1. The first step in defense of my hypothesis is to put forward the following thesis: The belief that something is appropriate for someone logically entails the belief that everyone concerned with the issue ought to believe the same. This is not to say that the same thing is appropriate for all people; but those who are concerned and knowledgeable ought to agree on what is appropriate for whom. Although this very complex thesis cannot be fully defended here, some of its argument points can be mentioned.

First, the thesis reflects the underlying claim that evidence for a belief has some objective status over against mere assertions regarding the belief. Therefore, if everyone understood a given set of categories couching a statement, even if they differed over the usefulness of the categories, they could agree about whether the evidence as defined by the categories tends to support or undermine the belief.

Second, although people may begin with different categoreal perspectives, even different structures of existence defining those perspectives, there are objective issues of enriching life that reward or negate those perspectives. Although each perspective defines the values it enjoys, and perhaps does so in a way that no value can be articulated outside some perspective or other, there is an immediacy to value-enjoyment that nudges the perspectives themselves. Otherwise there could never be a good reason for developing or altering any of the structures of existence. This parallels for concrete experience the point made about values for theories in Chapter Four.

Third, this thesis regarding the universality of a claim for appropriateness or truth derives from the Greek structure of existence, and therefore is parochial. But both Cobb and I accept it. However transmogrified, it seems to have survived the Greek perspective into the Christian, and to have appeal even to those structures of existence originating in India and China.

Whereas completed statements (systems and structures of existence) are by definition relative to their worlds, ongoing judgments are by definition partly outside the perspectives that provide their resources; mentality is not finished fact and, therefore, cannot be given completely definite position in a perspective. Only by choice or heedlessness can a judgment on a perspective repeat the criteria in the perspective itself. Contemporary people are right, therefore, in believing either that others ought to agree with them about what is appropriate for various subjects, or that evidence ought to be offered to warrant altering the original beliefs.

2. The second step in defending my hypothesis is to suggest that we live in a sufficiently unified world as to constitute a community of inquirers or spiritual pilgrims. Buddhists are making claims about what is appropriate as an existential structure for human beings, including Christians, and Christians make equally inclusive counterclaims. This point is presupposed in the very suggestion that structures of existence are genuine alternatives. If neither felt the others were their fellows or if the only communication were the hurling of anathemas, would there be no significant contradiction.

This step, coupled with the first, yields the conclusion that Christians, Buddhists and all other contenders ought to be looking for agreement on what structures of existence are appropriate for the various interested parties. This is not to say the same structure must be agreed upon as appropriate for all, only that they all agree on the just distribution. I am not at all sure that, in posing his options, Cobb means to suggest that Buddhism is right for some people, Christianity for others; but that would be a logically tenable position.

3. My third step is to point out that this logical possibility is not a historically real one. We simply live in too much a world society, defined by causal interactions if not roughly common culture, to accept that other people are to be humanly addressed according to radically different structures of existence.[4] If we were dealing not with structures of existence, but with skin color or even national heritage and ethnic identity, the relativity problem would not be so acute; in fact, that kind of diversity would add richness. But the issue as to structures of existence involves commitments regarding basic visions of reality, a point John Cobb has made as well as anyone. Choices regarding structures of existence are not merely cognitive matters, as might be implied if the discussion dealt only with the visions of reality. They also are choices in which the choosers take responsibility for the kind of human existence they make for themselves. This is as true of Muslims, Hindus, Buddhists, Taoists and Confucianists as for Westerners. Responsible structures of existence are what define people as human in relation with eath other. Other people's appropriate structures of existence should be seen as appropriate for them from the perspective of one's own structure of existence.

These three steps have been taken in defense of a thesis concerning a logical *ideal*. It would be "nice," from a rational point of view, if these universalistic considerations could be realized in the structures of existence aborning. Without them a world community is in grave difficulty, if not impossible. But the conditions for realizing the logical ideal simply might be absent. It might be the case that the only possibilities for making the various old structures of existence mutually relevant would involve abstracting them to the point they would become mere doctrines, lacking existential force. This would mean, in effect, that a person would have to choose one structure of existence or none, John Cobb's position, but not make up a new one out of many.

I want to argue against this, suggesting reasons why conditions do obtain for taking seriously the ideal of developing a new structure of existence both appropriate to the modern world and faithful in the main to the principal cultural traditions. The position should not be overstated. It cannot be argued, for instance, that somewhere the new structures of existence already lie in wait, although an argument from *esse* to *posse* is the strongest kind. Nor do I mean to suggest that the majority of the people in the world are on the threshold of a new structure of existence; my claim is only that the cultural leaders are the pace setters. Finally, I do not mean to suggest any certainty that the threshold will be crossed. On the contrary, various antagonisms might make it impossible. The abyss of savagery is particularly close in this age of nuclear war, economic and social injustice and the brutalization of nature. At the same time, the impetus to solve these problems fosters, and may indeed require, the development of the delicate but intense sensitiveness of a new structure of existence.

IV

The first argument for my conception of the present historical situation is a criticism of Cobb's model for the development of structures of existence. He traces the rise of the current panorama from primitive developments of conscious signals and unconscious symbols through the increasing entry of symbols and their conscious manipulation into consciousness. Axial people, centering the organizing principles of their experience in various foci of conscious life, arose across the globe in different guises. But, from this point, Cobb's hitherto genetic account of human nature becomes radically historical. Each kind of axial people developed in ways unique to their traditions so that, after two or three thousand years, we have the basically pluralistic situation affirmed in the long quotation on pages 118f.

Is this sudden historical diversity what we would expect for structures of existence? Probably not. Organized and deeply rooted historical diversity is to be expected when the environments within which peoples develop are different and reinforce different cultural artifacts. Geographic and climatic differences give rise to different historical routes where they bear upon cultural development. Particular historical decisions and events also form different environments from which historical divergence takes place. So, for instance, the tropical climate of India makes possible the religious style of the naked ascetic forest dweller, a style impossible in deserts or very cold climates. And the personalities of heroes and contingencies of holy places and events will differ from culture to culture. Admitting that these historical differences account for differences in *modes* of existence, to use Cobb's term, they seem not to be so powerfully relevant for determining the basic structures of existence.

The issue is whether the conditions, to which the development of a structure of existence is an evolutionary response, are massively inherited by all people simply by virtue of being human. Is there such a thing as "the human condition"? Or are the relevant conditions for a structure of existence the sort that are likely to be peculiar to particular cultures? This is an empirical issue, and I shall suggest evidence that the basic conditions are those massively inherited by all cultures.

Suffering is universal, although its forms may be idiosyncratic. Language is universal and, if Noam Chomsky is correct, even its basic forms are universal. Because suffering must be coped with and coping is expressed in language, the symbolic interpretation of suffering is close to the heart of communications that define human life in community. Furthermore, it seems universal that all peoples experience a conflict between their symbolic representations of the meaningful world and symbol-shaking intrusions. Suffering is the most poignant shaker of the domestications of life; but novelty, sharp endings and unexpected joys also call normal thinking into question. All primitive cultures have sacred ceremonies associated with suffering, birth, death, maturation and ecstasy, and axial cultures augment or replace these by philosophies and theologies, superinterpretations of the meaning of life's meanings. I argue, therefore, that not only do all peoples have structures of existence, they ideally can have structures of existence adequate to these universal conditions.[5]

V

Against this position it surely will be remarked that the universality of the creative development of structures of existence does not entail the development of a coherent structure of existence. There may be many adequate structures, and the diversity is to be understood as a matter of historical contingency. To meet this objection, a further argument is necessary concerning the universality of human response to the conditions occasioning structures of existence. My provisional suggestion is to sketch a brief model of the educable "parts of the soul" and then hang evidence on the model showing that each cultural tradition acknowledges and attends to all parts, with different emphases and historical forms.[6]

Plato in the *Republic* proposed the model of a soul with three parts, each with its own ideal virtue and appropriate form of education. The *appetitive* part of the soul consists of desires, affections and loves, each a vital response to some erotically attractive value. Movement in life comes from the impulse toward the erotic objects. The *rational* part of the soul deals with the discovery of patterns that make the desires compatible, distinguishing the better from the worse values and articulating an order of life according to priorities. Well-developed reason has dialectical ways of criticizing patterns of compossibility according to real values whose very discernment has been criticized. The *spirited* part of the soul is a kind of aggressive force integrating the other components. When desires are passionate and not feeble, and when reason is developed and critical, not second-hand or dull, spirit integrates the personality by seeing that the desires pursued are those guided by reason. As Plato put it, spirit can get angry at either one's desires or one's reason, whipping them into line. Plato's main point was that each of these parts of the soul has an ideal to fulfill, necessary for personal virtue. Desires must be passionate or there is a deficiency of life. Reason must attain to wisdom or there is a deficiency of possible ways of living, especially good ways in unjust circumstances. Spirit must attain to courage and discipline or the best intentions and the strongest passions will never meet to bear fruit.

Plato's three ideals for the soul illustrate three aspects of personal life that can be developed according to the abstract categories of the process model.[7] Desires correspond to the many data providing value and energy to the process, seeking new objectification. Reason corresponds to the function of mentality, providing conceptual propositions, including new ones, for subjective harmony. And spirit corresponds to the drive for unification, restricted by the "categoreal obligations," to use Whitehead's term, and perfected by the degree to which the richest desires (most valuable data) are incorporated in the wisest way for mutually enriching objectification. These ideals may not be the only ideals on this basic level. Perhaps the ecstatic "selflessness" of the ideals of the musician for the spirit, the prophet for the reason and the mystic for the heart are supplementary; and perhaps there are yet others. But Plato's parts of soul, with corresponding ideals, seem to be a useful empirical hypothesis.

Any structure of existence, I suggest, involves ideals for each of these parts (at least), and institutions for fostering them, because all parts are important for full human life. In Cobb's terms, each part is a "seat of existence" and, although the different cultural traditions emphasize and punctuate them differently, all are present. In religious terms, the ideal of spirit is discipline or personal integrity, the ideal of reason enlightenment and the ideal of desire perfect love.

The development of spirit appears at first to be discipline in the sense of gaining control over desires, thoughts and actions. Ascetic practices and disciplines are most obviously brought to mind in connection with yoga, whose stages of development have been carried over into Buddhism through which they met and reinforced meditative practices of posture, breathing and thought control in Taoism and Confucianism. Ascetic practices in Christianity likewise have involved physical and mental control, down to the days of the Methodist *Discipline.*

The first appearance of the development of spirit, however, gives way in all traditions to the recognition of a special blockage: the sense of self or ego. In the *Bhagavad Gita* the self-sense (*ahamkara*) leads people to identify several physical and psychological factors in the world as being "themselves" as opposed to "others," and the other things in the world are interpreted in terms of how they affect for good or ill the welfare of those egoistic selves. As a result, people's objective perceptions are distorted by selective vision, the motives of their actions are perverted by subtle self-seeking and their thinking is obsessed with the sufferings and triumphs of the fictional ego. Spiritual release consists in giving up attachment to and belief in the empirical ego. One's perfected perception then is undistorted, one's actions directed purely to the good of the end in view, and one's thinking empty of suffering and egoistic triumph. All happenings are the manifestations of God, simple and natural, and all things can be taken in stride. This theme is paralleled in the notion of nonaction in Taoism, pellucid sincerity in Confucianism, enlightenment or buddhi in Buddhism and chivalry in medieval Christendom. The hero of this kind of religious development is the warrior (Arjuna), who perceives and acts without ego, a pure expression of the essence of things, the samurai, the knight templar, the theocratic ruler.

Even the purest spirit without enlightenment is amoral and experientially unfulfilled. The universal emphasis on religious experience, on knowledge of the ultimately good and on mystical apprehension of the ultimate itself need not be documented. In some traditions such as yoga and certain forms of medieval Christian mysticism, the religious experience is connected with a process of discipline. Other strands of religious knowledge emphasize history and moral experience as the arena in which enlightenment is attained, strands often important in Judaism, Christianity and Confucianism. The sage gains enlightenment in many ways, and stands as a religious type alongside the warrior.

The development of religiously appropriate desires is another universal ideal. On the face of it, this means eliminating selfish and misplaced desires. Deeper, it means developing the passions that embody the divine life. Cobb is certainly correct that this element has received its greatest emphasis in Christianity and its best expression in the life of Jesus. Christianity stresses that all other religious virtues (discipline to surrender the self, enlightenment of all knowledge and faith) are nothing without love. Yet the perfection of the passions, and their articulation as love, is not exclusive to Christianity. It is of the essence of bhakti tradition in Hinduism, said to be the highest form of spirituality in the *Bhagavad Gita*. It is the main thrust of the theme of rectification of the will in Confucianism and, if the Taoists object to it, the reason is not a rejection of the ideal of *Jen*, love, but a rejection of the belief it can be attained by effort. Even the prophets spoke of the God who preferred love to the smell of burnt offerings; Jesus' rendition of the commandment in terms of loving God and man with all heart, soul and mind was a quotation from earlier sources. All religions have their saints, the lovers whose divine love has salvific power.

My general thesis now is that all axial structures of existence contain themes whose paradigms are soldiers, sages and saints. The structures differ by historical models, and they differ in the ways these are related. In some structures one paradigm may be dominant over the others; but the others are there and play essential roles. To live in such a structure is to define oneself by (at least) each of the ideals.

Now the problem for a contemporary structure of existence is to find appropriate new forms of the soldier, sage and saint. More particularly, the problem is to find a way of having these together so as to minimize loss of the old traditions and to maximize the intensity of cultural life in the context of the current environment. For the development of the new structure of existence, can we open ourselves to the resources of all the old ones, as an occasion (in process philosophy) enriches itself by broadening its world?

VI

Responding to an early presentation of this thesis, Professor Cobb does not object to the examples I have cited. Rather, he objects that the model presented does not register the uniqueness of the seats of existence peculiar to the different structures of existence but comes from a Western perspective. For instance, the model does not reflect the Indian attempt to establish the seat of existence in a consciousness outside the flow of empirical psychic life. It does not reflect the importance of aesthetic and rational distance for the Greeks. It does not emphasize the importance of the person and then the spirit as seats of existence in the Judaeo-Christian tradition. And particularly, it is insensitive to the Buddhist "quest for the cessation of all cravings."[8]

To this two reflective points can be made. I will try to show how each of these seats of existence is interpretable according to the model given and how, although they are emphasized differently in each tradition, they are all present to a degree. Then I will comment on the existential contexts in which integrations need to be made.

1. According to Cobb's account, the structure of the person arose in Israel as both reason and feelings were objectified and subordinated to personal responsibility. A person is one whose will is responsible for actions. This is to say, in terms of the Platonic model, that spirit (in Plato's sense) has attained a high de-

gree of integration, dominating the shape of one's desires and the use of intellect so that the spirit's own style articulates the person's identity. Aesthetic people's identity is articulated by what they see; rational people by what they know; spirited people by what they will in making themselves autonomous.

The Christian structure of existence as spirit objectifies even the will so as to make people indefinitely responsible for all components of their personality. But this is what one would expect from a high development of spirit in the Platonic sense. Spiritual persons are those who have attained personal freedom in the possession of their own will.

It should be pointed out that my model for rendering spirit is Plato's, the Greek who was the "author" of Socrates, in a manner of speaking. To say that Plato made reason the seat of existence, subordinating either spirit or eros (highly developed appetites) is to be mistaken about the texts, I believe. Holding a genuinely social conception of reality, Plato believed reason is the ideal of precedence when action throughout a complex environment is at stake. Spirit is the ideal, in the form of free personal integrity, when the individual is at stake and eros is the ideal when God's action in the world is at stake. According to Plato, God brings value into the world by having it loved.

Cobb argues that the Christian structure whose seat is in personal spirit is alien to the Indian attempt to seat consciousness outside the flow of events. Yet the fact that the method for spiritual development requires the same thing in both cases—the loss of the ego ("he who would save his soul must lose it")—suggests the difference is overdrawn. The warrior in the *Bhagavad Gita* who purges himself of self-sense, looking at all things from a conscious standpoint not identified with or attached to any of them, is the person who can act, faithfully valuing the relevant things and serving their intrinsic goods, regardless of reflection back on himself. Although Arjuna's center of consciousness is not identified with any time-bound psychic state, his identity as an actor is given in his situation and deeds, just as with a Western person. Furthermore, the principles integrating his actions are natural expressions of Krishna, not intrusions of his self-ish character. This is not so different from having the "mind of Christ."

It might be argued that Eastern persons or spiritual types do not identify themselves with their personal career, and that this identification is central to the Western notion of responsibility. Part of this argument may rest on metaphysical beliefs in the soul as an enduring lumplike substance. But both Cobb and I reject this in favor of a process view of the soul as a society of occasions. We would agree with process philosophy in that people's characters are the cumulative sets of forms each of their occasions presents. Bad spirits, corrupted by attachment to an ego-image, would be those overly concerned to reiterate some conception of their past character, and to filter their prehensions of the world through that image, in such a way as to sully what could be more richly prehended and to objectify a less than maximal posture. The development of spiritual discipline through loss of self enables a person's character to reflect growth in the realistic maximization of value throughout life without selfish distortions.

The boundaries of self and not-self are fluid and somewhat conventional. As suggested above, I would go beyond many process philosophers in stressing that individual responsibility entails that some past occasions involving commitment must function essentially, not just contingently, in responsible occasions. Minimal requirements for a personal responsible agent would be that certain acts in the past are essential components of the person's present commitments, to be accepted or rejected with moral responsibility. This helps in the understanding of individual responsibility in the Western metaphors, and helps also in making sense of the doctrine of karma. All in all, the process model of the responsible individual works as well for the Indian conception of the person as for the Western. Where the West stresses the responsibility in the continuities, the Indian tradition stresses the perfection of action in the moment. But neither side is lost to the other.[9]

From the Buddhist side, one of the chief points of contrast Cobb draws is that Buddhist love does not involve a self, a lover, and that there is no important distinction between the lover and the beloved.[10] In Christianity, on the other hand, while the ideal of love is equally high and noble, the emphasis is on developing the loving self. But just what is there in this difference?

The Buddhist would say the real self of each person is the Buddha-nature, and the Buddha-nature is the same for everyone.

What is loved, however, is not the Buddha-nature per se, but the other person as the expression of the Buddha; the ideal activity of love is to attempt to bring the beloved to a realization of the Buddha-nature. This is paralleled in Christianity by love of others as the creatures and vehicles of God the *logos;* the ideal activity of this love is to help the others realize the *logos* more purely. The Christian calls attention to the identity of the other developing through time, and speaks of the beloved's identity in terms of the beloved's time and space determinants. The bodhisattva's attention to disciples and beloved followers is equally concerned with the details, temporal and spatial, of their spiritual development. Where the Buddhist would say one must attend to the details of the beloved's individual character to foster the realization of the common Buddha-nature in the beloved, the Christian would say that one fosters the life of Christ in each disciple by attending to the development of the beloved's historical character. The Christian would stress the realization of discipleship in coming to terms with one's historical position. But what could say this more plainly than the Mahayana Buddhist doctrine that all things are empty except historical contingencies apprehended as such? Nirvana is samsara.

It is sometimes said that Indian spirituality locates salvation in flight from the concrete world of historical existence. Yet both Christians and Buddhists see that the only way to grasp historical existence for what it is lies in attaining to a kind of eternal consciousness in the moment, a divine perspective. Both agree the divine perspective is the most real in an ontological sense and both agree that the historical continuum is where the action is, literally. Some modes of Buddhism emphasize monastic withdrawal, but then so do the Trappists. Some modes of Christianity, especially medieval mysticism, interpret the eternal in the moment on the analogy of sexual ecstasy; Tantrism does the same. Both traditions have meditative strands, activist strands, devotional strands. Although the emphases differ and the mixes look different, similar components are to be found in both. And our present problem regarding the structure of existence is that the particular mixes in each case are inadequate to our times.[11]

Both the discussion above and Cobb's own discussion in *The*

Structure of Christian Experiences have been seriously remiss in suggesting that Christianity, Buddhism or, indeed, any of the great axial cultural traditions have clearly identifiable natures. There is no such thing as "the Christian" or "the Buddhist"; and it is very difficult to make generalizations about "Christians" or "Buddhists." There are many different kinds of each. I agree with Cobb in his recent statements that there is not even such a thing as an "essence" to a tradition unifying the historical variations.[12] The variations may be more important than the common features. Probably the desire to find something "essential" in a tradition comes from the will to invoke it as authoritative, or to identify an opposing position and finally refute it. What we identify as relevant in a tradition comes from the interests of our own perspectives, which brings the discussion to the second point.

2. As noted above, Cobb objects that the hypothesis about the parts of soul with their corresponding ideals is parochial and therefore cannot guide us toward an integrated structure of experience. The first response to that objection has been an empirical one, arguing that, well, yes it can. Such an empirical argument can never be more than suggestive, however. I want now to turn to consider the context in which developing a structure of existence is problematic for us, a theme introduced at the beginning of this chapter.

If our social lives were completely unproblematic, then perhaps the habits directly inherited from the cultural traditions of our local communities would be sufficient; or, if they were not, still we would not know what was being missed. But our social lives are extremely problematic. One of the areas of difficulty arises from the fact that economic, military, educational and environmental affairs, those dimensions of experience that are significantly shaped by religious expectations and images, involve people with different cultural inheritances. Since cultural life is not self-contained in museum form, it affects our larger social interactions. And, if those interactions are to be developed in deeply human ways, then cultural meanings need to be reflected in them. Cultures need to be appropriated not by isolated individuals but by individuals in interaction. It is the interactions that need to be given depth by culture.

Because our social interactions are worldwide, there are world-

wide, common pressures on the appropriation of cultural resources. It is not enough, then, for each person to bring his or her
cultural resources to the interaction, because the cultures, if wor-
thy, are not the individual's so much as the interaction's. Nor is it
enough to develop a style of social interaction that recognizes and
tolerates the diversity of others' cultures, because (although this
is minimally very desirable as the foundation of civilization) it
makes "culture" a private affair, somehow unimportant to the
public social interaction. If social interactions themselves are to
be given human meaning through taking on cultural significance,
then the locus of appropriating cultural resources is the interactions themselves. As John Dewey pointed out, experience is a
public affair, and so are structures of existence and problems of
constructing them. This is by no means alien to Whitehead's recognition that both persons and groups are "societies," with social
relations between them.

The situation is not that the historical traditions have independent moments that now bring them into tangential scrapes or col-
lisions. It is rather that our present lives, which need the
appropriation of cultural meaning, present new demands that no
single tradition can meet. If hereditary Christians interact with
hereditary Buddhists, then neither can find full meaning for that
interaction solely from their own inherited traditions without
treating the others as uncultured ciphers in the interaction. Moral
as well as practical pressures send us scurrying to find cultural
resources from many worlds.

If anything, our danger is that the common pressures of economic and military technology will homogenize our cultural appropriations. It will be difficult to stress the viability of diverse
cultural responses to common forms of interaction. But for the
moment it should be pointed out that the traditional structures of
existence shaping our world are limiting conditions as well as resources. If the intellectual or mental content were abstracted from
those structures, perhaps we could accept, reject, divide and re-
combine them as we do ideas. But, in fact, to abstract in that way
is immediately to leach out the existential power of those structures to enrich our lives on the most basic level. Even if we were
to do that we could not escape the existential hold those old

structures have on our lives. No matter what structure of existence I attain to, I will have gotten there as a Methodist from Missouri. There are some places a Japanese Buddhist can go I could never reach.

Nevertheless, the structures of existence currently established in diverse cultures are somewhat inadequate to the existential needs of contemporary culture. Each of the major religious traditions seems to be looking back to its own roots, and looking over to its neighbors', in preparation for large-scale developments. Surely the religious synthesis of Vedic and Dravidic cultures in the *Bhagavad Gita,* or Hebrew and Greek cultures in Augustine, were no more daring blends of apparent opposites than any of those contemplated now. We cannot simply will a new structure of existence into being. It arises through deep and mysterious historical processes.

But what we can exercise control over is the development of an appropriate vision of reality. Our control can be critical and dialectical. If we are careful not to confuse theoretical visions with existential structures, there is the possibility we may wisely influence the latter with the former. This point is one of the chief strengths of John Cobb's philosophical theology.

VII

One of John Cobb's special virtues is that he combines feeling for the concrete things of life with skill in abstract metaphysics. The main discussion of this chapter, however, has lain between these two, dealing with cultures and their interaction regarding the formation of structures of existence. It became clear in the last section that the concrete immediacies of social life are central and common components of the diverse problems of the mixed appropriations of cultures. It is now possible to point out reflectively that the abstract categories of metaphysics have also provided a common point. For it is by means of abstract categories that the problem of dialogue can be set up in the first place. The very vagueness of abstract categories, their capability of being instantiated in Buddhist ways or Christian ways, means they can provide common ground for understanding diversity.

Furthermore, if they are abstract enough, then debate about their validity or usefulness can take place cross-culturally without begging important intercultural questions.

One of Cobb's greatest contributions has been to employ the categories of process philosophy for the interpretation of the cross-cultural debate. They have been exhibited in the discussion so far. But just which of process philosophy's categories have been employed? Those of the natural cosmology, defining causation, individual existence in surrounding social environments. The categories defining process theism have not been employed. In fact, Cobb points out that the conception of God, defined by process theism, is *in*compatible with the Buddhist perspective, not a common ground for potential dialogue. He argues that whereas Christians stress ultimate things having to do with God, Buddhists stress other ultimate things having to do with the elimination of craving and with emptiness.[13] But if there are as many difficulties with the process conception of God as have been urged in the previous chapters, perhaps that catholic argument lacks force.

An argument could be made, however, that the conception of God the creator, indeterminate apart from creation, immanent in the determinate being of things within creation, is a more nearly neutral way of understanding "ultimate things." That, of course, is an argument for a different place.[14]

· VIII ·

Contributions of
Process Theology

I

Let us now retrace the steps of our critical argument. In Chapter Seven, through a discussion of John Cobb's theory of experience relative to fundamentally different cultures, it was claimed that there is a common immediacy to problems of social life and a common intellectual milieu that can be created by the abstract categories of speculative process philosophy. But it was also noted that among the process categories that might provide the context for discussion is not to be found the process conception of God. For God, conceived by process theism as distinct from creativity itself, is one way of expressing what is denied by the Buddhist tradition.

Is the process conception of God valuable within a more limited cultural sphere as a theoretical interpretation of the general Western tradition? Charles Winquist argues that process philosophy in general can be integrated with the tradition of transcendental philosophy; but in Chapter Six it was claimed that that case cannot be made out unless the essential character of transcendental philosophy is naturalized. In Chapter Five it was argued that the process conception of God itself has few if any advantages over more classical conceptions as an interpretation of directly Western experience.

Chapter Four argued that Charles Hartshorne's attempt to develop Whitehead's conception of God into a full-scale theological position is best with the paradox that the necessity in God must somehow transcend God as such, if God is to be a society. If God is not to be conceived as a society, but as a unitary actual entity, then the unity of God and the world, plus creativity, must somehow be understood. Chapter Three argued that Whitehead's "Category of the Ultimate" is incapable of solving the problem of the one and the many, framed this way. And Chapter Two argued that Whitehead's conception of God as a unitary actual entity, even when interpreted with the thoroughness and sensitivity of Lewis S. Ford, cannot be unified itself if God is conceived as relative to the world.

This brings the discussion back to Chapter One, which pointed out that Whitehead's chief contribution to philosophical theology was to separate the conception of God from that of creativity. The cumulative effect of our argument has been to suggest that much of Whitehead's process philosophy (that having to do with nature) is valid, but that there are grave difficulties with the conception of God. Perhaps, then, we should abandon the initial move of separating God from creativity.

But the conceptual hallmark of Whiteheadian process theology is to distinguish neatly between creativity and God. Hence the title of this book. Therefore I must begin an assessment of the contributions of process theology with an essentially negative statement. The previous chapters have argued in various ways that the separation of creativity from God has led to significant inadequacies for process theism in the following areas: ontology, God's presence in the world, the world's bearing on God and the presentation of a persuasive theistic hypothesis. The critical points can be summarized around these themes.

Ontology

If one accepts something like the ontological principle—that any complex state of affairs calls for an account by reference to the decisive actions that determine it—how can one account for the existence of the complex world described by process cosmology? The Category of the Ultimate locates the decisions whereby things within the world determine each other. But why is there the complex world in the first place? Or why is there the structure articulated by the Category of the Ultimate?

One might answer that the Category of the Ultimate is simply ultimate. David A. Pailin suggests something like this. But then if an exception to the ontological principle is made for this very important complexity, why not make exceptions elsewhere?

One might answer, as Lewis S. Ford does, by saying that God in the primordial creative act creates the metaphysical structures, including the Category of the Ultimate. But then that primordial divine act would not be bound by the metaphysical structures as other actual entities are, and God would thus be an exception to the system, a consequence Whitehead wanted to avoid. One might say that the primordial divine act *illustrates* the category of the ultimate by claiming that it reduces a plurality of otherwise unrelated eternal objects to a unified divine vision. But, since the Category of the Ultimate would still be a product of that primordial divine act, the act illustrates the category only by chance, not by the kind of necessity according to which acts are what they are by conforming to categoreal requirements. Furthermore, it is hard to see how the preenvisioned eternal objects could be disjunct from one another enough to illustrate the Category of the Ultimate if they are totally indeterminate with respect to each other.

One might answer, as Whitehead seems to have, that the ontological question is misplaced, that metaphysics provides only empirical generalizations of the sort in his categoreal scheme, and that the ontological principle extends only to decisions and complex results within the realm of actual entities. This answer may reflect an incorrigible sensibility about the nature of ultimate explanations. But if the questioning of complexity gives rise to the ontological principle, then the complexity of the cosmos's most basic structures forces the same issue.

One might answer, with Hartshorne, by shifting the center of gravity from a balance of creativity and God to a conception of God as totally inclusive of creativity, of the Category of the Ultimate and of any other needed metaphysical categories. Then through the ontological argument one might prove that God, including all contained within the divine nature, is necessary. Yet for the ontological argument to be valid it must be shown that the God thereby proved is conceivable or possible. Unfortunately, the conception of God as inclusive of the structures that provide the necessary divine nature cannot be made coherent.

I believe the ontological question can be answered only by conceiving every determinate complexity to be the product of a kind of ontological creativity not contained with the system of the world or explained by created categories. Whether ontological creativity can be related to a conception of God is, of course, another matter.

God's Presence in the World

By virtue of the medium of creativity, in Whitehead's hypothesis, God and finite actual occasions are subjectively distinct, although constitutively related to each other. Particularly, each finite occasion derives its subjective aim through a hybrid physical prehension of God's special valuational ideal for the occasion.

If God is a single actual entity, however, as Whitehead and Ford claim, then at no finite time can God objectify a valuational ideal to be hybrid-physically prehended. Furthermore, it is difficult to conceive how God as a single entity could prehend the immediate antecedents of a finite occasion in order to construct the valuational ideal, if the dates of the finite occasion's antecedents are always simultaneous with the everlasting divine concrescence.

If we say, with Hartshorne and others, that God is a society of occasions, then the above difficulties are avoided. But in what does God's nature as divine consist? Each divine occasion is divine *because* it conforms to the requirements of divinity; this suggests, however, that those requirements are normative in a way that is not reducible to the structures that are illustrated in the various members of the divine society. The transcendent normative reality of these requirements for divinity would seem to be more divine than the mere actual enduring individual. In fact, the society which is God is inexorably necessitated always to do the best, to remember without loss and so forth, a necessitation finite occasions escape by virtue of their imperfect illustration of categoreal conditions.

However it is that God is conceived to present a valuational ideal to each finite occasion as its subjective aim, it is alleged that this kind of divine presence allows room for human freedom. What an occasion does with the subjective aim given among its initial data is a function of the occasion's own *sui generis* creative process. Compared with the other initial data, however, the divine lure is more encompassing, dictates its integration more thoroughly and results from an infinitely deep background of already having influenced the other initial data. This is the point to which process theologians appeal in commending divine providence. But, with regard to freedom, a person is less free from God's lures than from anything else among given data; the ability to alter subjective aim within the process of concrescence is trivial, less by far than the ability to reject or alter more ordinary initial data. Rather than regard God's presence in the world as sufficiently limited so that people can be free over against God, the better strategy would seem to be to conceive God's presence as coincident with people's freedom and characterize freedom as a function of relations within the world.

The World's Bearing upon God

One of the virtues alleged for process theism is that it represents God as capable of being moved by the world, particularly, to be sensitive to human feelings and initiatives. How is the world present in God?

Assuming that it is possible to surmount the difficulties in conceiving of a divine prehension of a finite occasion, what of the finite realm can be prehended? The only things that exist to be prehended are the objectified satisfactions of the finite occasions. Their subjective processes of coming-to-be are not available to be prehended. Therefore, God cannot know us as we are in our hearts, where that means the subjective immediacy of our own concrescence. Yet religious intuitions have it that we are present to God in our inmost being.

Now it may be granted that the subjective form of concrescence is objectified in one's satisfactions, except for those elements eliminated before satisfaction. Our own sense of the continuity of consciousness from one moment to the next derives from our hybrid physical prehensions of our own past states that have significant mentality in their objectified subjective forms. The process deity could therefore feel us as we remember ourselves, indeed with no loss of fact or tone in memory. Yet memory is always of what has passed away; precisely what cannot be remembered is the present immediacy that constitutes the heart of our inmost reality. We may be present in God as memories but not as our own subjective immediacy. It may be preferable to say that our own spontaneous immediacy, as well as our prehended pasts, are products of an ontological creativity that has no character except that of its products; in this case our immediacies would *be* the divine character.

The Theistic Hypothesis

As a philosophical theology, process theism claims to present an hypothesis about the nature of God that is adequate to the demands of at least some of the theistic traditions. These demands include internal consistency and coherence, applicability to a world well formed by science and secular culture and adequacy to the experiential depths of the religious traditions. If the previous critical points have some substance, however, their force is to cast grave doubt on the consistency, coherence, applicability and adequacy of the process conception of God, at least in its versions that have been analyzed here. If theism is true, it is not true in the process form.

Perhaps, then, one might inquire into whether the conception of ontological creativity I have been urging as an alternative to process theism is closely enough connected to the Western religious traditions to be adequate to their important intuitions and to warrant the name God. Although there is justification for connecting this to certain Western mystical traditions, it must be admitted that this hypothesis also has close affinities to Eastern traditions not often regarded as theistic. Perhaps this is a quasi-theism, and is warranted. Perhaps it is as unwarranted as the hypothesis of process theism. Perhaps some other theistic hypothesis is preferable. Perhaps the theistic traditions are simply wrongheaded. As far as proof goes, the situation is very open.

II

Now the extraordinary historical contribution of process theology has been to put us in the position to inquire theologically with the freedom illustrated in the last paragraph. This is manifest in at least three areas: the nature of speculative theology, the relation of theological inquiry to tradition and the cultural context of theological inquiry itself.

1. By formulating its conception of God as an abstract hypothesis, process theology has made it incumbent on every contender in the theological arena to engage in speculative theology. In

order to see whether one's conception agrees or disagrees with process theism, still more to argue that it is preferable, one must formulate one's view as an alternative hypothesis. Of course the meaning of hypothesis varies from position to position, and so does the nature of understanding and explanation. With these also vary the relations of the hypotheses to logic and experience. Once engaged in the speculative endeavor, however, one's hypothesis must be expressed through an internal critique of the alternatives. Process theism is the first twentieth-century alternative necessary to be engaged by any conception of divine things, first by virtue of temporal priority in the contemporary world, and first by virtue of the elegance, clarity and thoroughness of its exposition.

Speculative theology is the formation and warranting of abstract theological conceptions by means of argument. Although the nature of argument is itself always vulnerable in a theological discussion, the logical status of moves in speculative theology is similar to that in play. And therefore it has the objectivity of being nothing other than what it is—positions more or less well formed and warranted by such and such arguments. Of course there are enormous emotional and intellectual biases stemming from prior experience and commitment, biases that as matters of contingent fact cannot be transformed into arguments. Furthermore, theology includes a great many other enterprises than its speculative component. But speculative theology as such is a thoroughly public enterprise, and the personal biases of its practitioners are not private rights but public liabilities.

2. Not only by its reestablishment of speculative theology, but also by its practice, process theology has brought greatly needed correctives to the relation of theology to the various religious traditions. Process theology emerged during the years when, among Christians, theology was usually thought to be a service discipline for the practice of religion. Neo-orthodox protestant theology was explicitly "dogmatic" or "kerygmatic," concerned with finding ways to state the gospel to be preached. Roman Catholic theology still reflected the distinction between natural and revealed theology; but even its natural theology, for instance in the work of Maritain, was concerned with the modernization of the Roman Catholic theological tradition. These forms of theology were not fully public, however, because in their appeals to revelation to

warrant propositions they failed to address each other with evidence.

Like protestant liberalism and Boston personalism, process theology saw theology as objective, public inquiry. But it went far beyond those movements in articulating a new logic for theology. Instead of theological propositions being expressions of a deposit of faith, they can be regarded as hypotheses for articulating and interpreting the resources of experience, particularly that of the religious traditions. Process theologians have analyzed explicitly the viability of process theological conceptions to represent the depths of experience and allow it to be appropriated. Parallel to the developing objectivity in hermeneutics that has allowed the study of Scripture to be a cooperative venture of scholars regardless of backgrounds and commitments, process theology has developed techniques for assaying the conceptual viability of traditional and experiential claims. Whereas before it was usually thought that one's background was normative for one's theological inquiry unless one converted, now it is recognized that one's background is the special resource and limitation one brings to inquiry but is not a commitment to the result of inquiry. Inquiry thus is free.

Of course this has been a hard message for professional theologians to accept. It clearly relativizes "belonging" to a religious tradition. John B. Cobb expresses the point with greatest courage and clarity:

> Still it is true that this relativism relativizes also Christianity as a whole. Christianity as a whole is conditioned in particular ways that necessarily render it incomplete, unclear, and distorted. To commit myself unqualifiedly to Christianity would be inconsistent with a full recognition of the inadequacy, unclarity, and distortion of the beliefs through which I identify myself as a Christian. But to be a convinced Christian is not incompatible with this recognition. I am a convinced Christian because I have experienced the system of Christian beliefs as generally surviving well through encounters with alternatives. I am continuously engaged in testing their capacity for further reformation through these encounters. I will remain a convinced Christian unless and until I have encounters that force me to break with this process of continuously reforming Christianity and adopt a fundamentally different approach.[1]

3. As reflected in John Cobb's words, the cultural context for theology is the whole plenum of the world's religions and the antireligious secular traditions. Of all the modern theological movements originating from within Christianity, process theology has been most explicit and effective in bringing its cultural heritage into dialogue with alien perspectives. Cobb's own views discussed in Chapter Seven are but one example. One reason for the pioneering lead of process theology is that the conception of nature in process cosmology is far more resonant with non-Western conceptions of nature than are most other forms of Western philosophy. But another reason is the recognition by many process theologians that non-Christian religions are genuine alternatives and that one has not asserted one's own view until one has asserted it with reference to those alternatives.

A practical result of this recognition of the world-cultural context for theology is that the best institutions for theology are universities in which the world's religions are presented with as much philological and hermeneutical objectivity as possible. Particular religious institutions are no longer the home of theology. Theology with a traditional institutional label, for instance "Methodist theology," or even "Christian theology," is less public, more partial, tentative and incomplete than theology needs to be. This is a revolutionary consequence, both for universities and for church institutions.

That the cultural context for theology is worldwide does not simplify its task or provide it with a new authority. Consider the following problem. In the Western religious and intellectual traditions it has usually been thought that the proper understanding of a person takes the form of a story. One's identity is one's story and, without understanding how the elements of one's life play roles in stories, one is grasped as something less than human. Yet for the Buddhist tradition the form of the story is usually an illusion, an attempt to project unity onto a person that is not there. Episodes are to be chronicled, and the parts of life set in their various environments. But the perspective of a unified consciousness presupposed in the coherence of a story is illusory. This is a fundamental divergence of traditions. Which is right? How would one tell? What does it mean to be right? Need one choose, or are there simply (at least) two ways of "understanding"? The meaning of "ultimate things" and salvation depends upon these issues.

The questions indicate something of the extraordinary breadth and depth of theological inquiry. Translation and interpretation of sources, cross-cultural comparisons, the cultivation of spiritual practices and the attempt to provide fruitful but discriminating intellectual categories are all necessary components for addressing these issues. It may be noted parenthetically that process theology is nicely neutral with respect to the two sides in that dispute, and thus can provide an intellectual map of the terrain, as it can in many issues. But it must be noted as more to the historical point that process theology has been the major influence to bring such crucial questions for civilization to public discussion.

In light of these considerations about the historical importance of process theology, my objections to its conceptual structure are pale. Although I believe the process conception of God cannot be sustained in critical scrutiny, its speculative impetus need not be lost with the abandonment of that particular theistic conception. The philosophical cosmology of which process theology is a part is a rich enough matrix to nurture other and perhaps more viable conceptions of God.

Chapter Notes

Preface

1. From "The Development of Process Theology," in *Process Philosophy and ChristianThought*, ed. by Delwin Brown, Ralph E. James, Jr., and Gene Reeves (Indianapolis and New York: Bobbs-Merrill, 1971), p. 46.

One

1. For a justification of this approval of Whitehead's general approach to nature and causation, see my *Cosmology of Freedom* (New Haven: Yale University Press, 1974), esp. chap. 2; chaps. 4-6 detail some of the amendments I would make to Whitehead's cosmology. For a critical discussion of how this approach gets along without Whitehead's conception of God, see Donald W. Sherburne's review of *ibidem* in *Process Studies* 6/4 (Winter 1976), 279-92. See also Sherburne's own "Whitehead Without God," in *Process Philosophy and Christian Thought*, ed. by Delwin Brown, Ralph E. James, Jr., and Gene Reeves (Indianapolis and New York: Bobbs-Merrill, 1971), pp. 305-28.

2. A. N. Whitehead, *Religion in the Making* (New York: Macmillan, 1926), pp. 158-60.

3. A. N. Whitehead, *Process and Reality: An Essay in Cosmology* (New York: Macmillan, 1929), pp. 521-24.

4. Ibid., p. 528.

5. Lewis S. Ford, "The Viability of Whitehead's God for Christian Theology," in *Proceedings of the American Catholic Philosophical Association* 44 (1970), p. 141.

6. Ibid., pp. 142-44.

7. For Whitehead's "categoreal obligations," see *Process and Reality*, chap. 2. Acceptance of the categoreal obligations is of course general and "in principle"; they are somewhat problematic in themselves and would

have to be made consistent with a conception of process without Whitehead's God.

8. This is the thesis of Chapter Three.

9. For a systematic elaboration of this alternate conception of God, see my *God the Creator* (Chicago: University of Chicago Press, 1968); for a more complete discussion of God's presence in cosmological process, see my *Soldier, Sage, Saint* (New York: Fordham University Press, 1978), chap. 5.

10. See Whitehead, *Process and Reality*, p. 74.

11. I have explored this independently in *Soldier, Sage, Saint*, chap. 5; *God the Creator*, chap. 4; "Creation and the Trinity," in *Theological Studies* 30 (March 1969), pp. 3–26; and "Can God Create Men and Address Them Too?" in *Harvard Theological Review* 61 (1968), pp. 603–23.

12. Whitehead, *Process and Reality*, p. 522.

13. In this regard, see also Ford's "Whitehead's Categoreal Derivation of Divine Existence," *Monist* 54/3 (July 1970), pp. 374–400. Ford's rebuttal to my argument, further elaborated in Chapter Three, is in "Neville on the One and the Many," *Southern Journal of Philosophy* 10/1 (Spring 1972), pp. 79–84; my rejoinder is loc. cit., pp. 85–86.

14. Whitehead, *Process and Reality*, pp. 341 and 347.

15. For an interesting discussion of St. Thomas Aquinas from a Whiteheadian perspective, see Lewis S. Ford's "Whitehead's Transformation of Pure Act," in *The Thomist* 41/3 (July 1977), pp. 381–99.

16. See Kant's *Critique of Pure Reason*, B 72, trans. by Norman Kemp Smith (London: Macmillan & Co., 1933), p. 90.

17. The argument was developed by Lewis S. Ford in an unpublished essay; despite its ingenuity, it has difficulties, some of which are cited below, and Ford has not followed up on the argument.

18. Whitehead, *Process and Reality*, p. 38.

19. Ibid., p. 434.

20. "Two Types of Philosophy of Religion," in *Theology of Culture*, ed. by Robert C. Kimball (New York: Oxford University Press, 1959), pp. 10–29.

21. Whitehead, *Process and Reality*, p. 469.

22. See Ford's "Whitehead's Conception of Divine Spatiality," in *Southern Journal of Philosophy* 6/1 (Spring 1968).

Two

1. See Ford's central article, "The Non-Temporality of Whitehead's God," in *International Philosophical Quarterly* 13/3 (September 1973), pp. 347–76; see also his "Whitehead's Categoreal Derivation of Divine

Existence," *Monist* 54/3 (July 1970), pp. 374–400; "Whitehead's Conception of Divine Spatiality," in *Southern Journal of Philosophy* 6/1 (Spring 1968), pp. 1–13; "The Duration of the Present," in *Philosophy and Phenomenological Research* 35/1 (September 1974), pp. 100–6; and "Genetic and Coordinate Division Correlated," in *Process Studies* 1/3 (Fall 1971), pp. 199–209.

2. See his "On Genetic Successiveness: A Third Alternative," in *Southern Journal of Philosophy* 7/4 (Winter 1969), pp. 421–25.

3. Ford quotes A. N. Whitehead, *Process and Reality: An Essay in Cosmology* (New York: Macmillan, 1929), p. 342.

4. This argument is similar to the suggestion discussed earlier in Chapter One, sections III and IV.

5. Ford, "Genetic Successiveness," p. 422.

6. Ibid., p. 423.

7. A. N. Whitehead, *Interpretation of Science*, ed. by A. H. Johnson (Indianapolis and New York: Bobbs-Merrill, 1961), p. 241.

8. Ford, "Genetic Successiveness," p. 424.

9. Whitehead, *Process and Reality*, p. 28f.

10. Ibid., p. 29.

11. See Ford's "The Non-Temporality of Whitehead's God."

12. He did say that "in the first place, God is not to be treated as an exception to all metaphysical principles, invoked to save their collapse. He is their chief exemplification" (*Process and Reality*, p. 521).

13. On this topic, see Ford's "In What Sense Is God Infinite? A Process Perspective," in *The Thomist* 42/1 (January 1978), pp. 1–13.

14. In *Cosmology of Freedom* (New Haven: Yale University Press, 1974), chaps. 4–6, I discuss a conception of process that eliminates Whitehead's doctrine of subjective aim, noting the emergence of spontaneity. In *Soldier, Sage, Saint* (New York: Fordham University Press, 1978), chap. 5, spontaneity is analyzed as the presence of the creator.

15. This theme is developed in my "Metaphysical Argument for a Wholly Empirical Theology," in *God: Knowable and Unknowable*, ed. by Robert J. Roth, S.J. (New York: Fordham University Press, 1972).

16. Knowledge of the creator and freedom of human response are treated in my essay, "Can God Create Men and Address Them Too," in *Harvard Theological Review* 61 (1968), pp. 603–23; the distinction between the world as the terminus of the divine creative act and the world as an integral whole apart from God is treated in my "Creation and the Trinity," in *Theological Studies* 30/1 (March 1969), pp. 3–26. Ford responds to these points in "Can Freedom Be Created," in *Horizons* 4/2 (1977), pp. 183–88.

Three

1. *Process and Reality* (New York: Macmillan, 1929), p. 168.
2. Ibid., p. 36 and *passim*.
3. Ibid., pp. 36 and 68.
4. Ibid., p. 74f.
5. Ibid., pp. 75 and 41.
6. Ibid., p. 5.
7. Ibid., p. 31,
8. Ibid., p. 32.
9. Ibid., e.g., p. 47.
10. Ibid., p. 46.
11. Ibid., p. 30.
12. Whitehead wrote:

In other words, philosophy is explanatory of abstraction, and not of concreteness. . . . Each fact is more than its forms, and each form "participates" throughout the world of facts. The definiteness of fact is due to its forms; but the individual fact is a creature, and creativity is the ultimate behind all forms, inexplicable by forms, and conditioned by its creatures. Ibid., p. 30.

13. Ibid., p. 67.
14. Lewis S. Ford has responded to an early statement of the arguments of the last three sections in his "Neville on the One and the Many," in *Southern Journal of Philosophy* 10/1 (Spring 1972), pp. 79–84. Generally put, his defense is that Whitehead's category of the ultimate can be supplemented by saying that God in the primordial creative act creates the determinate character of eternal objects by envisioning them in relation, and that satisfies my argument for an ontological creator. In my reply, "Response to Ford's 'Neville on the One and the Many' " loc. cit., pp. 85–86, I note that eternal objects prior to divine envisionment need not be said to exist at all since they are completely indeterminate, and that God needs to create the concreteness of the actualities as well as their possibilities, since it is only by virtue of relevance to concrete entities that the eternal objects can be graded in divine envisionment. My original article, Ford's response, and my counter-response are being reprinted in a volume called *Explorations in Whitehead's Philosophy*, ed. by Lewis S. Ford and George Kline (New York: Fordham University Press, forthcoming).
15. My early attempt to formulate this view can be found in *God the Creator* (Chicago: University of Chicago Press, 1968), chaps. 5 and 7.

Four

1. Charles Hartshorne, *Creative Synthesis and Philosophic Method* (LaSalle, Ill.: The Open Court Publishing Co., 1970).

2. Ibid., p. 257f.

3. Hartshorne interprets eternity as "everlastingness," and therefore loses the sharp model contrast with becoming, expressed for instance in Whitehead's or Tillich's philosophy. Furthermore, for Hartshorne, the concrete becoming includes the abstraction of being without remainder. This makes the situation a "degenerate third" because the opposition or "secondness" between eternity and becoming is reduced to mere qualitative difference—ever-presence versus sometimes-presence.

4. Hartshorne, *Creative Synthesis*, p. 91f.

5. Ibid., p. 118.

6. See Weiss's *Modes of Being* (Carbondale: Southern Illinois University Press, 1958), pp. 42–45; see also his *Man's Freedom* (New Haven: Yale University Press, 1950), pp. 3–11.

7. Hartshorne, *Creative Synthesis*, p. 177.

8. See, for instance, Weiss's early discussion in *Reality* (Princeton: Princeton University Press, 1939), chap. 5; see also "Process and Substance: A Reply," in his *First Considerations* (Carbondale and Edwardsville, Ill.: Southern Illinois University Press, 1977), pp. 223–37.

9. Hartshorne, *Creative Synthesis*, p. 195.

10. Perhaps Hartshorne's most sustained defense of this point is in *The Divine Relativity: A Social Conception of God* (New Haven: Yale University Press, 1948), chap. 2, "God as Absolute, Yet Related to All."

11. Hartshorne, *Creative Synthesis*, pp. 190 and 198ff.

12. See my *Cosmology of Freedom* (New Haven: Yale University Press, 1974), chap. 3, for a defense of this Platonic position.

13. For a brilliant articulation of the "eternity" of Platonic forms as possibilities, see David Weissman's *Eternal Possibilities: A Neutral Ground for Meaning and Existence* (Carbondale and Edwardsville, Ill.: Southern Illinois University Press, 1977).

14. Hartshorne, *Creative Synthesis*, p. 59.

15. See *The Collected Papers of Charles Sanders Peirce*, vol. 6, ed. by Charles Hartshorne and Paul Weiss (Cambridge, Mass.: Harvard University Press, 1935), pars. 35–65.

16. Cf. Ford's "Whitehead's Categoreal Derivation of Divine Existence," in *The Monist* 54/3 (July 1970), pp. 374–400.

17. David A. Pailin, "Neville's Critique of Hartshorne," in *Process Studies* 4/3 (Fall 1974), p. 194.

18. Ibid.

19. Many of the best of his discussions are collected in Charles Hartshorne, *Logic of Perfection and Other Essays in Neoclassical Metaphysics* (LaSalle, Ill.: Open Court Publishing Co., 1962).

20. Pailin, "Neville's Critique," p. 194.

21. Ibid., p. 195.

22. See Hartshorne's "Three Strata of Meaning in Religious Discourse," in *The Logic of Perfection.*

23. Hartshorne, *Creative Synthesis*, p. 236f.

24. Pailin, "Neville's Critique," p. 188.

25. Ibid.

26. Hartshorne, *Creative Synthesis*, pp. 75–82.

27. Pailin, "Neville's Critique," p. 191.

28. Ibid., p. 196f.

Five

1. *The Reality of God* (New York: Harper and Row, 1966).

2. See Tracy's *Blessed Rage for Order* (New York; Seabury, 1975).

3. Ogden, *Reality of God*, p. 44. Ogden is the author of *Christ without Myth: A Study Based on the Theology of Rudolf Bultmann* (New York: Harper & Row, 1961); this book has made him a major figure in the American theological movement interested in hermeneutics.

4. Ogden, *Reality of God.*

5. See my *Cosmology of Freedom* (New Haven: Yale University Press, 1974), chap. 1.

6. Ogden, *Reality of God*, p. 17; as an aside, it seems to me that consistency is entailed as a necessary condition *by the nature of truth*, not by secularity; Ogden's claim suggests an ideological interpretation of logic.

7. He does not try to refute the moral limitations directly, but his argument that moral action implies belief in God clearly is his answer. I shall deal with the epistemological problem here.

8. Ogden, *Reality of God*, pp. 12–20.

9. Ibid., p. 23.

10. See my *God the Creator* (Chicago: University of Chicago Press, 1968), pp. 229–44.

11. Ogden, *Reality of God*, p. 24.

12. Ibid., pp. 30–35.

13. Ibid., p. 39ff.

14. Ogden defines God as the ground of our confidence, and it does not make sense to him to say that the confidence might be groundless (ibid., p. 38f). Even on the reflective level, there is only the problem of *how* God's reality is to be conceived, not whether there is such a thing.

15. On the whole question of Ogden's argument for the unavoidability

of faith, see Antony Flew's review of his book in *The Journal of Religion* 48 (1968), pp. 150–61. Although Flew is remarkably ill at ease when dealing with metaphysical issues and criticizes Ogden insensitively there, his criticisms of several other points are interesting. In the same issue (pp. 161–81), Ogden reviews Flew's book, *God and Philosophy*, and gives as good as he gets.

16. Ogden, *Reality of God*, p. 47.

17. Ibid.

18. Ibid., p. 48.

19. Ibid., p. 47.

20. Ibid., p. 58.

21. Ibid., p. 17.

22. Ibid.

23. Ibid., p. 230.

24. Ibid., p. 57.

25. In the citation given by Ogden, Whitehead said: "The subjectivist principle is that the whole universe consists of elements disclosed in the analysis of the experiences of subjects" (*Process and Reality* [New York: Macmillan, 1929], p. 252). The qualification "reformed" has to do only with the form of primary experience; the reformed principle says we experienced a stone as "this stone as grey" rather than as "this sensation of greyness" (ibid., p. 242ff.).

26. Ogden, *Reality of God*, p. 57.

27. Ibid., p. 58.

28. Ibid., p. 62.

29. Ibid., p. 175.

30. See the previous chapter and also Hartshorne's *Divine Relativity* (New Haven: Yale University Press, 1948), p. 143f. Hartshorne tries to escape the argument I give by saying that actuality is limited but possibilities as such are unlimited, and therefore by implication not transcendent of actualities. But possibilities cannot be unlimited since they distinguish what is possible for this actuality from what is impossible. And insofar as possibilities are partially indeterminate (e.g., it is possible for one to stand up or remain seated) they cannot be contained in actualities that are completely determinate (e.g., one cannot contain sitting-or-standing in only sitting, and possibility contains both sides of the disjunction).

31. A more classical theory identifying divine knowledge with a divine act of creation that is immediately present to whatever reality things might have, processive or otherwise, at least might have its heart in the right place.

32. See Ogden, *Reality of God*, pp. 166–74.

33. Ibid., p. 180.

34. Ibid., p. 177ff.

35. Ibid., pp. 188–205.

36. Ibid., p. 201.

37. Ibid., p. 220.

38. Ibid., p. 177.

39. It is not clear what this participation has do to with love, although its metaphysical meaning is apparent.

40. Ogden, *Reality of God*, p. 226.

41. Ibid., p. 230.

42. Ibid., 226.

43. Ibid., p. 224f. See Whitehead's *Adventures of Ideas* (Cambridge: Cambridge University Press, 1933), pp. 366–81.

44. Ogden quotes this in *Reality of God*, p. 218.

45. Ibid., p. 228f.

46. See ibid., pp. 99–119.

Six

1. Charles E. Winquist, *The Transcendental Imagination: An Essay in Philosophical Theology* (The Hague: Martinus Nijhoff, 1972).

2. Ibid., p. 5f.

3. See, for instance, Cobb's *A Christian Natural Theology Based on the Thought of Alfred North Whitehead* (Philadelphia: Westminster Press, 1965).

4. Winquist, *Transcendental Imagination*, p. 3.

5. In this regard, see Winquist's more recent *Communion of Possibility* (Chico, California: New Horizons Press, 1975).

6. Winquist, *Transcendental Imagination*, p. 39.

7. Ibid., p. 18.

8. Ibid., p. 24f.

9. Ibid., p. 31.

10. Ibid., p. 36.

11. Ibid., p. 36f.

12. Ibid., p. 51f.

13. Winquist's discussion is in ibid., p. 75.

14. A. N. Whitehead, *Modes of Thought* (New York: Macmillan, 1938), p. 57.

15. Winquist, *Transcendental Imagination*, p. 77.

Seven

1. *The Structure of Christian Existence* (Philadelphia: Westminster Press, 1967). Cobb derives the terms and basic axial analysis from Karl Jaspers' *The Origin and Goal of History* (New Haven: Yale University Press, 1953).

2. Cobb, *Structure of Christian Existence*, p. 148.

3. "A New Christian Existence," *Neues Testament und Christlische Existenz*, ed. by H. D. Betz and L. Schohroff (Tübingen: J. C. B. Mohr, 1973), pp. 79–94.

4. Cobb makes a very useful distinction between structures of existence and modes of existence. The modes are various ways of embodying the larger structures. For instance, there are ancient, medieval, modern, Catholic, Protestant and Orthodox modes of Christianity, each expressing the life of spirit. Distinctions between structures of existence are much more radical, defining human life in very different ways. To be happy in a world society with different structures of existence is to say people are human in a different sense from the way we are. To accept different modes of a single structure of existence is only to say there are different ways of expressing a common humanity. I myself have some reservations about the genus-species way of distinguishing structures and modes, preferring kinship relations and family resemblances; but for the present point it is adequate.

5. A very fine extended account of the problem mentioned in this paragraph is John E. Smith's book, *Experience and God* (New York: Oxford University Press, 1968), esp. chap. 6.

6. This position is expanded in my *Soldier, Sage, Saint* (New York: Fordham University Press, 1978).

7. By "process model" I mean that generally composed of the themes articulated by Whitehead. Cobb discusses the model in detail in *A Christian Natural Theology* (Philadelphia: Westminster Press, 1965), esp. chap. 2 and 3. Another version is in my *Cosmology of Freedom* (New Haven: Yale University Press, 1974).

8. See *John Cobb's Theology in Process*, ed. by David Ray Griffin and Thomas J. J. Altizer (Philadelphia: Westminster Press, 1977), p. 162.

9. The impact of Western ideas of evolution on Indian thoughts has brought to the surface a far more historical expression of the Indian conception of life than is found in the ancient texts. Nevertheless, recent writers, for instance Sri Aurobindo and Sri Krishna Prem, have carefully reinterpreted the traditional texts in historically-oriented language. A comparison of Aurobindo's philosophy with Teilhard's would indicate that the issues distinguishing India and the West are not strictly bifurcated over the importance of concrete historical life.

10. Cobb, *Structure of Christian Existence*, p. 139.

11. Cobb's treatment of the differences between structures of existence curiously downplays the role of different orientations to God. Perhaps this is because a discussion of orientations would quickly turn to a discussion of theories about God.

12. *John Cobb's Theology in Process*, p. 169f.

13. Ibid., pp. 150–54.

14. See, for instance, my "A Metaphysical Argument for Wholly Empirical Theology," in *God Knowable and Unknowable*, ed. by Robert J. Roth, S.J. (New York: Fordham University Press, 1973).

Eight

1. In *John Cobb's Theology in Process*, ed. by David Ray Griffin and Thomas J. J. Altizer (Philadelphia: Westminster Press, 1977), p. 168.

Name and Subject Index

DATE DUE

OC 22'84			